EACH ONE
WIN ONE

stan toler and louie e. bustle

a complete strategy for effective personal evangelism

D0874926

BEACON HILL PRESS
OF KANSAS CITY

Copyright 2006
by Beacon Hill Press of Kansas City

ISBN 978-0-8341-2239-0

Printed in the
United States of America

Cover Design: Chad Cherry
Interior Design: Sharon Page

Library of Congress Cataloging-in-Publication Data

Toler, Stan.
  Each one win one : a complete strategy for effective personal evangelism / Stan Toler and Louie Bustle.
    p. cm.
  ISBN-13: 978-0-8341-2239-0 (pbk.)
  ISBN-10: 0-8341-2239-1 (pbk.)
  1. Witness bearing (Christianity) 2. Evangelistic work. I. Bustle, Louie E. (Louie Elvis), 1942- II. Title.

  BV4520.T65 2006
  248'.5—dc22

                                                                              2006029683

10 9 8 7 6 5 4 3 2

The authors wish to dedicate this book to the memory of Dr. Bruno Radi.

Dr. Bruno Radi went to be with the Lord on Tuesday, June 21, 2005. He was a missionary, statesman, and evangelist.

Bruno gave his heart to Jesus when he was 11 and was called to preach as a teenager. He began his studies in the Bible Institute in Buenos Aires and started preaching when he was 16. His first ministry assignment was in the northern part of Argentina where he started the work with the Toba indigenous people. Bruno served in many different roles in the church: pastor, district superintendent, field director, evangelism director of South America, and then regional director of South America.

Dr. Radi also had a great impact on the broader church of Jesus Christ. While he was pastoring a strong, growing Nazarene church in Rosario, Argentina, he also worked for 10 years coordinating evangelistic campaigns all across Latin America for Luis Palau. His vision for leadership and passion for evangelism had a major impact on church planting and the multiplication of the Kingdom across South America and in many other countries around the world.

Bruno was a leader, a mentor, and friend. We will miss him greatly, but we know his legacy will continue to impact the church for years to come. He was God's giant.

"I know where I am going, but there are millions who don't—keep on telling them" (Bruno Radi).

—Louie Bustle
—Stan Toler

CONTENTS

About the Authors   6

Acknowledgments   7

Introduction   9

How to Use and Apply This Book   11

  I. Strategy   13
    1. The South American Strategy   15
    2. A Biblical and Historical Strategy   23
    3. The Jesus Strategy   31

  II. Preparation   37
    4. Each One Win One   39

  III. Discipleship   45
    5. The Big Brothers and Big Sisters Model   47
    6. Prayer Cells   52

  IV. Harvest   61
    7. Evangelistic Campaigns   63
    8. Multiplying Churches and Pastors   69
    9. IMPACT: Coordinating the Plans   76

  V. Leadership   85
    10. Goals and Leadership   87

Appendixes   97
  Appendix A: Leader's Guides   A1
  Appendix B: Student Outlines   B1
  Appendix C: Each One Win One Checklist   C1
  Appendix D: Follow-up Checklist   D1
  Appendix E: Big Brothers and Big Sisters Checklist   E1
  Appendix F: Insights into Spiritual Gifts   F1
  Appendix G: Prayer Cell Checklist   G1
  Appendix H: The Evangelistic Campaign Checklist   H1
  Appendix I: My Top 10 Commitment List   I1
  Appendix J: Big Brothers and Big Sisters "Top 10" Checklist   J1
  Appendix K: Poster—Each Church Plant One Commitment   K1
  Appendix L: Poster—Each One Win One Commitment   L1
  Appendix M: Certificate—Soul Winner (accomplished)   M1
  Appendix N: Certificate—Soul Winner (commitment)   N1
  Appendix O: Certificate—Church Commitment   O1
  Appendix P: Sermon Text—"Harvest Now"   P1
  Appendix Q: Membership Class Outline   Q1

Notes   191

ABOUT THE AUTHORS

Stan Toler is senior pastor of Trinity Church of the Nazarene in Oklahoma City. For several years he taught seminars for INJOY Group—a leadership development institute. He has written over 50 books, including his best-sellers *God Has Never Failed Me, but He's Sure Scared Me to Death a Few Times; The Buzzards Are Circling, but God's Not Finished with Me Yet; The Five-Star Church;* the popular Minute Motivators series; and his latest book, *The Secret Blend.*

Dr. Louie Bustle is the director of World Mission, Church of the Nazarene. He is married to the former Ellen Phillips.

The Bustles received their bachelor's degrees at Trevecca Nazarene University. Dr. Bustle also earned a master's degree at Nazarene Theological Seminary in Kansas City. In 1987 Dr. Bustle was given an honorary doctorate by Trevecca Nazarene University in Nashville.

Louie and Ellen served their first term as missionaries in the Virgin Islands. Following their first furlough, they were appointed to the Dominican Republic and were given the responsibility of opening the work of the Church of the Nazarene in this Caribbean country. Dr. Bustle served the Dominican Republic as mission director and the first district superintendent. He was involved in church planting and evangelism, as well as construction projects that included many Work and Witness teams. Ellen worked closely with her husband in mission activities.

In 1982, Dr. and Mrs. Bustle transferred to Peru where he served as mission director for one year. In 1983, Dr. Bustle was appointed regional director for South America, where he served until 1994. In February 1994, Dr. Bustle was elected by the General Board to serve as director of the World Mission Department.

Dr. and Mrs. Bustle have two children and a granddaughter. Their daughter, Beth, a nurse, is married to Rick Guilfoil and they have a four-year-old daughter named Amber. The Bustles' son, John, is currently a student at Kansas University Medical Center. The Bustles reside in Shawnee, Kansas.

ACKNOWLEDGMENTS

Special thanks to Jim Williams, Jerry Brecheisen, Annette Ferrell, Pat Diamond, and Deloris Leonard and also to Bonnie Perry, Barry Russell, and the entire Beacon Hill team.

INTRODUCTION

It is with great pleasure that we present *Each One Win One* to the church community. As authors, our desire is to spread the gospel of Jesus Christ to a needy world that is desperate for the message of hope.

Someone recently stated that 96 percent of churches do not have an identifiable witnessing plan in place. Our prayer is that you will be inspired, convicted, challenged, and then motivated to adopt the Each One Win One program in your local church. In Matt. 28:18-20, Jesus gave the Church a divine mandate that has never been rescinded. This Great Commission calls us to take the message of salvation to our friends and neighbors in order that we might win our world for Jesus Christ. We believe *Each One Win One* is an effective way to richly help you fulfill this calling.

Serving Christ and His Church,
Louie Bustle and Stan Toler

HOW TO USE AND APPLY THIS BOOK

The authors recommend the following steps in getting organized in your local church with the *Each One Win One* program.

1. Organize a prayer team to intercede to God on behalf of this outreach endeavor.
2. Appoint a team leader to lead this vital ministry in your church.
3. Select a ministry action team to give oversight to this new outreach endeavor.
4. Focus on the mission of your church.
5. Determine to plant a church.
6. Establish a Big Brothers and Big Sisters program as outlined in this book.
7. Schedule a community outreach program involving the entire church.
8. Praise God daily for the harvest of souls that He will bring into your church.

In addition, consult the appendixes in the back of the book for ideas to help you design your own certificates, posters, brochures, and other items for promoting and maintaining your program. The student outlines and leader's guides are especially useful for a small-group study or seminar presentation. Another excellent resource (also included) is the DVD featuring Louie Bustle. In it Dr. Bustle provides the biblical basis, overview, and scope of the plan. Recorded in both English and Spanish, this is an inspiring visual introduction to *Each One Win One*.

I.
STRATEGY

① THE SOUTH AMERICAN STRATEGY

The Church of the Nazarene has been ministering in South America for approximately 100 years. The years of planting the seed were long and difficult. Pioneer missionaries often faced intense persecution, and many of them gave their lives to present the gospel to those who had never heard it. But their commitment, experience, and evangelistic fervor brought about an explosion of growth that still continues.

The statistics speak for themselves. After 70 years of labor, the Church of the Nazarene in South America reported 18 districts, 349 organized churches, and 19,000 members. This is a respectable level of growth. But after implementing an aggressive plan of multiplication, the church grew to 39 districts, 883 organized churches, and 60,000 members—all in less than 10 years.

Now some could say, "South America is different from our continent. We could never do that here." However, God has used the same strategies to advance the church in the larger cities of North America and Europe as He did in the cities of South America. These strategies also work in rural areas. Pastors in the United States are just one example of those who are starting to use them with great success.

These strategies are simple and biblical. They were used in the rapid growth of the Early Church and will work anywhere they are prayerfully and properly implemented. Let's take a look at these 10 strategies that characterized God's work in South America:

1. A NEW MENTALITY

God gives us new light not only on living a holy life but also on developing new spiritual communities—communities that will practice holy living. The mind-set of the Early Church was on growth, both spiritually and numerically. Acts 16:5 says, "So the churches were strengthened in the faith and grew daily in numbers." Thus spiritual commitment and growth resulted in numerical growth.

In the 18th century, the spiritual-growth mind-set of John and Charles Wesley influenced their fellow students at Oxford University and set in motion the Methodist movement. Their method—with its small-group Bible study, prayer, fellowship, and discipleship—influenced scores of people in the 18th century, as it still does in the 21st. Once again, the result of spiritual growth was a growth in numbers.

The global efforts of the Church of the Nazarene began in the same way. Men and women committed themselves to personal spiritual growth, which resulted in the advancement of the Kingdom.

As all these servants of Christ—the Early Church, the Wesleys, and the pioneer Nazarenes—grew spiritually, they were intensely motivated to do all they could to lead others to Christ. They had a spiritually refreshed mind-set—a new mentality—that energized their efforts to expand numerically. They weren't afraid to use new methods to reach new people for the Kingdom. They had a mind like Paul:

> Though I am free and belong to no man, I make myself a slave to everyone, to win as many as possible. To the Jews I became like a Jew, to win the Jews. To those under the law I became like one under the law (though I myself am not under the law), so as to win those under the law. To those not having the law I became like one not having the law (though I am not free from God's law but am under Christ's law), so as to win those not having the law. To the weak I became weak, to win the weak. I have become all things to all men so that by all possible means I might save some. I do all this for the sake of the gospel that I may share in its blessings *(1 Cor. 9:19-23)*.

Paul was willing to use a new plan to reach *as many as possible* with the message of the gospel. That's what happened in South America. The Lord gave new light, and the church walked in it. New plans evolved out of a new mind-set, and rapid growth resulted.

South American Christians believed that Jesus wanted the church to make an impact on the continent—no matter what. They began to expect growth from every Christian, pastor, and church. But it became more than a goal; it became a way of life. They were no longer content with the same percentages. They wanted the Holy Spirit to move through their lives in a new way to reach lost souls and build the kingdom of God on earth.

Actually, their "new mentality" wasn't new at all. It went *back* to the teachings of the New Testament. Just like Paul, they were employing new methods to reach every person possible. They changed their minds from an *exclusive* mentality to an *inclusive* one, giving authority and responsibility to all who were willing to be involved in impacting the continent. Believing that "God does not show favoritism" (Acts 10:34), they mobilized *all* Christians—regardless of education, income, or nationality. They involved believers in winning new believers!

2. A PLAN OF MOBILIZATION: EACH ONE WIN ONE

Total participation must become a priority. For example, the church in the Dominican Republic used the program Each One Win One (which we will cover later). The goal of this program is to involve all of the members of the church in fulfilling the biblical principle found in Acts 1:8: "But you will receive power when the Holy Spirit comes on you; and you will be my witnesses in Jerusalem, and in all Judea and Samaria, and to the ends of the earth."

The church printed posters (see Appendix L) with the phrase Each One Win One and distributed them during a district assembly. In that assembly, reports showed 436 members in the church. According to the program's goal, during the year the pastors were to plant new churches and the Christian laypersons were to win new persons to Christ. Each pastor was encouraged to sign a promise of faith saying that with the help of the Lord, he or she would begin a new church that year (see Appendixes K and O). Members of the district were encouraged to return to their local churches filled with vision and enthusiasm to win the lost. They also promised to disciple their converts and bring them into the membership of the church.

Following the assembly, denominational leaders preached in each of the churches, challenging each member to win one new person to the Lord during the year; and they were also encouraged to sign a poster, promising to do just that. This resulted in an astounding number of people wanting to sign up.

During the next district assembly, it was reported that 557 new members had joined the church. Not only had the membership more than doubled, but 10 new churches had been organized as well. Imagine the atmosphere in that assembly as pastors reported victories won! They were reliving the Book of Acts!

The marvelous part about using the Each One Win One plan is that it is so simple everyone can get involved. New believers understand—and participate. And those who have been "sitting in the pew" for years have their excuses eliminated.

Each One Win One is a plan for the entire Christian community. It includes pastors, new converts, and those who have been believers for many years. Sometimes those who have been in the church for many years have few social contacts outside the church. This plan will enlarge their list of friends who do not attend church. The opportunities are endless. They can form friendships with persons who visit the church, with those in the workplace, and even over the phone.

Since new converts usually have many more contacts in the world outside the church, Each One Win One is a natural plan for them. Others have seen their transformed lives and are asking with the Philippian jailer, "What must I do to be saved?"

3. THE POWER OF OUR WITNESS

Rapid church growth begins with enthused believers sharing their faith with others. When the church mobilizes its members to share their experience, it turns into a spiritual epidemic. South American believers began to share their experiences with others in their community. And the church grew as a result.

Believers do not need to have extensive theological training to be effective witnesses. God blesses those who simply share their faith in a spirit of concern for others. They are bridge builders from the church to the world.

It is the *personal* relationship of the believer that best influences the lost. After surveying almost 1,000 unchurched people, the Barna Research Group concluded that in order for the church to reach these people, "someone in their midst will have to make the Christian faith real for them."[1]

We've seen it work in our own lives. Through the loving concern of a *godly pastor*, a father accepts Christ as his personal Savior. Through the change in *his* life, *another* becomes interested in the gospel. Then through the invitation of the *father*, that person accepts Christ as *his or her* personal Savior. This gospel chain of *one reaching one*, in a spirit of real-world faith, has resulted in scores of lost souls being won into the Kingdom.

George O. Hunter III expressed it this way in his book *To Spread the Power:*

When Christians report the chief characteristic of their human bridge in the discipleship, the two most cited adjectives are: caring and loving. Other adjectives are somewhat synonymous: encouraging, concerned, accepting, understanding, supporting, warm, affirming, sensitive, kind, and so on. Others report admirable or inspiring traits, like committed, believable, credible, patient, happy, fulfilled, honest, alive, friendly, humble, consistent, reasonable, authentic, stable, Christ-like, positive, reliable, faithful.[2]

Hunter also believes, "About half of all evangelical Christians have difficulty recalling anything their human bridge said that made the difference."[3] He says that the key to the ministry of evangelism is not *programming* but *participation*. Believers must simply express what God has done in their lives and be concerned that other persons become like Christ.

Especially in such an impersonal society, many people have a desire for someone to love them and to be interested in them. Each One Win One gives believers such an opportunity to show love and interest. And especially when the *whole church* expresses that love and interest, it produces an atmosphere that will help the unchurched feel welcome and want what the church has to offer. A growing church identifies with the needs of new people and preaches the gospel in such a way that sinners can find salvation.

4. AN EMPHASIS ON NATURAL GROWTH

The church grows on the basis of ministry, not money. That's how the church in South America grew—believers gave without thought of return. They were intent on increasing the Kingdom by adding new believers. One of the most important factors in the fulfillment of the Great Commission is the natural growth of the church. Many Christian leaders have been taught that growth happens in direct relation to the amount of money that is spent. They say, "If you give us *more money*, we will achieve *greater growth*." That mind-set does not die easily. But it must!

The New Testament church in Macedonia didn't have a large bank account, but it had a heart that was rich in ministry—and this resulted in an aggressive influence. Paul writes in 2 Cor. 8:1-5:

> And now, brothers, we want you to know about the grace that God has given the Macedonian churches. Out of the most severe trial, their overflowing joy and their extreme poverty welled up in rich generosity. For I testify that they gave as much as they were able, and even beyond their ability. Entirely on their own, they urgently pleaded with us for the privilege of sharing in this service to the saints. And they did not do as we expected, but they gave themselves first to the Lord and then to us in keeping with God's will.

The enemy wants us to think that growth is hard to produce, that we must depend on economic resources—a greater *program* to attract people from other churches and better *facilities* to attract a materialistic world. But God has given us light at this point. The church doesn't grow because of its resources; it grows because of its Source—the Holy Spirit. Zechariah 4:6 says, "This is the word of the LORD to Zerubbabel: 'Not by might nor by power, but by my Spirit,' says the LORD Almighty."

Aggressive church multiplication in South America did not depend on outside resources, not even district funds. It depended on the power of the Holy Spirit working through the lives of people in the local church—people who had a deep concern for the lost; people who were willing to give of their personal resources; people who were willing to reproduce their Christian life in the lives of others and bring the lost into the Kingdom.

The New Testament church wasn't a subsidized church; it was a sanctified church. It was set apart, called out to be a beacon of light to a darkened world. The churches described in the Book of Acts met in houses, not elaborate worship centers. Their leaders were not trained seminarians; they were bivocational men and women with a heart for ministry.

That gives us the biblical pattern for extending the church. We must not attempt to grow the church by mere economic means. We must grow it *naturally*, by spiritual means! We do not want to return to the old system of dependency (subsidy). It was that dependency that kept us from organizing more than one or two churches each year. Today, the natural growth of the church has become the standard. It is wonderful to live with the New Testament spirit, expecting wonderful things from God and attempting great conquests for Him!

5. THE INFILLING WITH THE HOLY SPIRIT

The principal foundation of the South American movement has been the clarion call that every believer be filled with the Holy Spirit. God's willingness to transform believers, cleanse their hearts from sin, and give them the power to witness for Christ has always been our message. However, there must be a renewal of its emphasis.

Pastors must preach this marvelous message with confidence and passion. They have been doing just that in South America, and the result has been the accelerated growth of the church in that region. It is a Spirit-filled church movement.

6. A SPIRIT OF GIVING

The change of mentality mentioned earlier also challenged South American believers to raise their level of vision from themselves to the world. They became committed to building the kingdom of God, not the kingdom of individuals.

South American Christians have a spirit of giving. When they give, God gives them abundant joy and blessing. God has broken the spirit of selfishness. In the past, pastors pleaded, "Lord, don't take that young person who has been called to preach and put him in another church. He is my right hand." Today, pastors have a different spirit and are willing to give up their *gifted* people to build the kingdom of God, rather than just their own church.

As a result, people have captured the vision of not only building the local church but also building their district, other districts in the same country, and districts around the world. Something has happened to them. They have begun to support one another and have become united. God is using them in the movement.

Aggressive church multiplication begins with an accelerated spirit of giving! God can bless such a program as Each One Win One when its leaders have a greater interest in building the Kingdom than in building their individual reputations.

7. THE POWER OF THE TEAM

Team spirit was another important aspect of the movement. Pastors had ministry teams in their local churches and a willingness to share their teams with other pastors to plant new churches. Pastors in large cities were joining hands, working together as a united force to reach the entire city. Pastors from other cities paid their own way to come to a neighboring city to help with a church's special emphasis. Laypersons caught that vision and joined in the strategy, working in a united spirit to build the kingdom of God.

The pastors and laypersons developed an evangelistic network, carrying out campaigns in each local church during a period of three months. They also had campaigns in house churches, citywide campaigns, district campaigns, and campaigns on the national level. There were teams doing outreach—preparing the location, coordinating the services, and discipling converts.

One of the examples is the Ecuadorian community of Puyo-Shell. With 30,000 people, there are 7 churches. The pastors had a goal of planting 20 more churches and worked together to reach it. They supported the evangelistic campaigns in each church and worked as a team to hold campaigns in various parts of the city, with the goal of planting new churches in those locations.

8. EMPOWERING THE LAITY

The total mobilization of laypersons and pastors required another mind-set change. Supervisors had to place the church in God's hands. That meant there would be less control on their part. They found they could give guidance through inspiration, without having so much direct supervision or regulation.

When people are allowed to use their own (leader-inspired) initiative, they will often respond spontaneously with Kingdom-building efforts. Their sense of worth has increased. Their confidence has been built. The leadership is still supervising, still motivating, but the workers are doing their own thing—they're ministering with their own God-given gifts, using their unique personalities to reach people for Christ.

District leaders encouraged and even expected pastors to plant churches. Pastors entrusted their laity with the growth of the church. Leaders supervised and challenged the church, but they told their people, "This is your responsibility: Go and make disciples." Today, pastors and laypersons are starting churches all over South America.

That rapid growth constantly calls for new pastors, new leaders—new disciplers. What are the results? The laity is mobilized to become leaders of the new congregations, pastors are developing and entrusting new leaders in systems of church growth, and the church is becoming the church!

9. A CALL TO TAKE UP THE CROSS

Emphasis on sacrifice and vision has also been a motivating force of the movement. The South American church believed in sacrifice! Like the first disciples, they felt joyful being considered worthy to suffer insult and reproach for the love of the name of Jesus (see Acts 5:17-42). The devotion of these Christians in South America compares in some ways to the dedicated devotion of the first disciples. They were willing to sacrifice everything for love of the Kingdom.

This call to sacrifice included the challenge of beginning churches without money. Many pastors gave sacrificially from their own pockets to start new churches. Laypersons moved to areas where churches did not exist and started churches in their homes.

In Peru, where many churches were started in this way, there are now 400 churches and the Church of the Nazarene is one of the largest denominations in the country. Others gave sacrificial offerings. The tithe, for many in the region, is only a minimum. Many South Americans donated their time in work groups to build churches. In one year, in the city of Bogota, Colombia, with its high cost of living, four properties were donated for church sites. With that spirit of sacrifice, it is not surprising that God started an evangelism explosion.

10. DECENTRALIZING THEOLOGICAL EDUCATION

Another key factor in the South American movement has been theological education by extension. The church has taken the seminary to the people. Those who have felt called to preach in South America can now participate in a program of theological education close to their homes. This method of training pastors and leaders has resulted in a constant resource of trained pastors for the growth of the church.

Previously, there were 200 students in residence seminaries. Now there are 2,600 studying in programs by extension in South America. Besides the educators that serve on an international level, the church is developing educators at the national, district, zone, and local levels, as well. As a result, many people have entered the ministry who in the past would never have had the opportunity to gain a ministerial education or to become a pastor of a local church.

This system of offering regional ministerial training is having an effect throughout the Church of the Nazarene. Bible classes and ministerial courses, coupled with pastors mentoring other pastors and laypersons trained in ministry, are flourishing today. This advice to a son in the faith is inspiring scores of new ministers—and ministries: "Do your best to present yourself to God as one approved, a workman who does not need to be ashamed and who correctly handles the word of truth" (2 Tim. 2:15).

Opportunities to let people begin second careers as ministers of the gospel have resulted in new church plants, added staff, and exciting outreach ministries. And what is the outcome of all this? Aggressive church multiplication.

These are thus the 10 activities/factors that have characterized the movement of God in the South American church:

- Developing a New Mentality
- Mobilizing All Believers (A Plan of Mobilization: Each One Win One)
- Sharing Experiences (The Power of Our Witness)
- Encouraging Natural Growth
- Preaching the Infilling with the Holy Spirit
- Increasing a Spirit of Giving
- Working as a Team (The Power of the Team)
- Supervising and Inspiring (Empowering the Laity)
- Sacrificing (A Call to Take Up the Cross)
- Decentralizing Theological Education

These are methods of ministry that are simple and cost little or nothing. They can be utilized anywhere in the world—even in your community. And through God's power they can result in a mighty movement of Kingdom building. The reason they are so successful is that they are based on a philosophy that is straight from the pages of the Book and the history of the Church—as we'll explain in the next section.

② A BIBLICAL AND HISTORICAL STRATEGY

Accelerated church multiplication isn't new. Its roots are in the Old Testament. Principles found in the earliest pages of history were adapted by the New Testament Church and, in turn, were passed along through the ages of Church history.

In the Book of Acts, we see how the Holy Spirit worked through the disciples and the first believers to plant and build churches—with inspiring results:

- The Church multiplied quickly, from 120 to 5,000 believers (4:4).
- The Church was a united (6:7).
- The Church grew daily (9:31).
- The Church's influence was far-reaching (11:21).
- The Church was Scripture-honoring (12:24).

The apostle Paul followed the same course in his mission. Wherever he went, he pointed people to Christ, discipled them in their faith, trained them for leadership, and then used their Spirit-anointed abilities to plant churches. The work continued long after he departed because he set up a strategy for accelerated church growth—a strategy that we are following yet today.

That work is seen in our own denomination. As we read about the early days of the Church of the Nazarene, we are challenged by the pioneers who went everywhere reaching the lost, discipling believers, training leaders, planting churches, and establishing districts. Pastors and laypersons founded the church to spread the message of the infilling and empowering of the Holy Spirit. The responsibility for the task was not only the district superintendent's but every member's as well. Each one sought to fulfill the Great Commission in planting churches throughout the world.

We've already seen the results in the churches of South America. In addition, when this biblical system of growth was begun in 1982, an explosion of new churches resulted. In the nine-year period from 1982 to 1991, 850 churches were planted—bringing the total to more than 1,200 organized churches. The system is effective because it is based on God's Word and is proven throughout the history of the Church.

STRATEGIES THAT IMPACT THE WORLD

Aggressive church multiplication is simply an extension of biblical methodology. Through this biblical strategy, we not only catch the vision of Old Testament and New Testament leaders but also want to spread it!

Our goal is to impact the world. But how? Here's the strategy in a nutshell:

1. Mobilize Christians to impact *individuals* by winning them to Christ, one at a time.
2. Mobilize Christians to impact *neighborhoods* through small groups (prayer cells).
3. Mobilize Christians to impact *communities* (plant new churches).

4. Mobilize Christians to impact *cities* (evangelistic campaigns).

5. Mobilize Christians to impact an *entire region, or country,* by developing church planters and planting new churches.

In the remainder of this chapter we will present biblical and historical strategies that can impact the world for Christ. It all begins with a promise! Acts 1:8 says, "But you will receive power when the Holy Spirit comes on you; and you will be my witnesses in Jerusalem, and in all Judea and Samaria, and to the ends of the earth."

God has given us a promise—a powerful promise, an eternal promise, a promise not diluted by the dilemmas of time, a promise greater than enemy regimes. He has promised the strength and power of the Holy Spirit for world evangelization. We cannot overemphasize that this is the source of our power. The Lord told His disciples not to set out on this task until the Holy Spirit was upon them. Without the promise, they would fail. With it, they would turn the world upside down (which is exactly what was reported of them!).

BY THE BOOK

Our strategies for church multiplication must be based on the principles of God's Word. In His Word God has given us not only the promise of His Spirit's power (Acts 1:8) but also the promise of His Spirit's guidance. John 16:13 says, "But when he, the Spirit of truth, comes, he will guide you into all truth. He will not speak on his own; he will speak only what he hears, and he will tell you what is yet to come." The Counselor—the Holy Spirit—not only guards Kingdom work but also guides it.

Throughout time, God has strengthened and led His people to accomplish His purpose by the wisdom of His Word. That inspired and authoritative insight is available to every leader. Within its pages God's appointed servants model the best leadership qualities for those who would follow. Let's look at a few of these stellar examples and insightful ideas:

1. The Example of Moses

According to the biblical account, Moses was the leader of about 600,000 men (not counting their families) who had left Egypt with him. As anyone knows who has led 600,000 people (or less), the task is both time-consuming and tiring. In fact, just getting a consensus for the time and place of a committee meeting would even make Job jittery!

For once, the in-laws had the best advice. When Moses' father-in-law, Jethro, saw him sitting at his desk in the desert, with a line of 50 to 70 persons waiting for him to solve their problems and to act as their judge, he knew something had to be done. Making judgments over stolen cows and borrowed pastures for 50 to 70 people at a time took more wisdom and strength than any one man could muster—even Moses.

In one of the first leadership training seminars in history, Jethro gave Moses a great Power-Point presentation. He advised Moses, "You will only wear yourself out. The work is too heavy for you; you cannot handle it alone. . . . Select capable men from all the people—men who fear God, trustworthy men . . .—and appoint them as officials over thousands, hundreds, fifties and tens" (Exod. 18:18, 21). The power was in the point.

With effective results, Moses accepted Jethro's advice and appointed the first pastoral staff! Looking at the following illustration helps us understand the scope of Moses' leadership. And it's easy to see that Moses' organizational skills were directed *internally.*

Moses

⬇

600 Leaders of 1,000

⬇

6,000 Leaders of 100

⬇

12,000 Leaders of 50

⬇

60,000 Leaders of 10

Moses modeled good leadership by creating an internal structure that churches still utilize. In many denominations, *internal* leadership effectively directs the *external* ministry. In the Church of the Nazarene, for example, there is an excellent internal organization. On the average, there is a leader for every 10 members (Sunday School teachers) and for every 50 members (presidents of auxiliaries and departments). For every 100 members, there is a pastor, an evangelist, or a missionary. And for every 1,000 members, or more, there is a district superintendent.

2. The Need for External Leadership

However, internal leadership alone will not cause the church to impact the world. This is the reason why many churches do not grow. They only think in terms of leadership within their four walls. The world is outside! Leaders must be prepared to take the message of the gospel to the streets. The Lord commanded us to "go and make disciples of all nations" (Matt. 28:19). The true purpose of the church isn't about refreshments and internal upkeep. Its true purpose is about recruitment. It gathers together for strength training. That strength is then used to take the gospel message to the sidewalks and pathways of the world.

What is the aim of your leadership? Is it directed toward internal maintenance or external impact? New Testament leaders emphasized both. Leadership in the Early Church stood out mainly because of its strong internal organization. Facing overwhelming opposition on both the political and religious fronts, men and women of faith rose to leadership prominence. Dedicated and daring leaders, like James and John or Priscilla and Aquila, recruited, trained, and motivated equally dedicated and daring fellow believers to impact their communities and their world. But when you think of New Testament church leaders, one stands out:

3. The Example of Paul

Born again from a life of religious rituals and regulations to a life of freedom in Christ, Paul borrowed from the disciplines of his previous religion to give direction to those who followed him freely in service to Christ. He modeled leadership excellence.

In Paul's letters we discover that the aim of his leadership was not just to grow churches but also to grow other leaders. He says to Pastor Timothy, "You then, my son, be strong in the grace that is in Christ Jesus. And the things you have heard me say in the presence of many witnesses entrust to reliable men who will also be qualified to teach others" (2 Tim. 2:1-2).

Notice his strategy. *First, Paul never wavered from his priority—exalting Christ:* "Be strong in the grace that is in Christ Jesus." Church multiplication isn't just about buildings, staff, curriculum, and long-range plans. It's about exalting Christ. It's about living in His resource, honoring Him in life and ministry, and lifting Him up in every activity. It's about pointing to Him as the only cure for what ails the soul. At Christmas, church folk often say, "Jesus is the reason for the season." For first-century Christians, exalting Jesus wasn't seasonal. He was the reason for everything—all the time. It must be the same today. Christ must be lifted up, above everything else.

The second part of the strategy—his plan—was to mentor others: "The things you have heard me say . . . entrust to reliable men." Paul's experiences of faith had a short shelf life. They weren't to be hoarded but shared. All along the way—from the road to Damascus to Mars Hill—Paul used his own ministries as object lessons to teach other believers how to be strong in life and leadership.

The third part—his method—was equally important—develop additional leaders. Spiritual experiences were entrusted to reliable believers "who will also be qualified to teach others." To the Early Church, Christianity was not a club but a cause. It believed that the entire planet needed to know about a Savior who could give hope to the hopeless and healing to the hurting. It was the church's job to duplicate knowledge and training in the lives of others.

Paul was into numbers—the number of developing leaders. In Rom. 16, Paul sends greetings to *27* leaders. In the last verses he mentions the names of *8* leaders who are with him. In another chapter, *35* leaders are counted as fellow workers of the apostle. "We count numbers, because numbers count," the ecclesiastical adage goes. Paul liked to count numbers when they related to multiplying leadership and planting churches.

We also read Paul's advice to Titus: "The reason I left you in Crete was that you might straighten out what was left unfinished and appoint elders in every town, as I directed you" (v. 5). Paul's strategy was to continually develop leaders of leaders, giving them responsibility and motivating them to do the same thing in the lives of others. He was developing *external* leadership—just as Jesus did.

In following Jesus Paul could find no better role model, and neither can we. Clearly, of our three examples, we have left the best for last. No one in history has equaled the leadership qualities of the Galilean. He led with His life. He led with His words. He even led with His silence. Everything He said or did was a perfect model to those who were motivated to build the kingdom of God on earth. He was the greatest leader of all.

4. The Best Leader of All—Jesus

Jesus' leadership stands alone in the annals of time. Unlike Moses, His leadership wasn't limited to a certain number (600,000). Unlike Paul, Jesus didn't have to make a midlife course correction. And unlike Moses *and* Paul, He didn't have a long career to create a strategy that would make the greatest impact. He only had three years. Three years! In three years, Jesus of Nazareth did everything that needed to be done to start a movement that would last forever. He impacted the world.

How did Jesus' leadership do this? He used a strategy that was different from that of Moses. In the beginning, Jesus did not have a following, but He began to develop leaders. Conversely, Moses had a following but he did not have leaders. It's often the same in the church. There are churches that do not grow because they only have leaders at the internal level. The key is to raise leadership at the *external* level, whose goal is to impact the world.

The purpose of *internal* leadership is maintenance. *External* leadership has as its purpose the moving forward of the internal organization—growth. Jesus focused on developing *external* leadership. He began with 12 apostles (Matt. 20:17, internal). Later, He had 72 disciples (Luke 10:1, internal). There were 120 in the Upper Room (Acts 1:15, external). Then there were more than 500 who saw the Lord (1 Cor. 15:6, external).

His strategy was successful. By the Day of Pentecost, 3,000 are mentioned (Acts 2:41). Farther on, 5,000 converts are counted (4:4). Soon it was getting harder to keep count. The Bible speaks of "more and more" (5:14). Finally, the ushers couldn't get an accurate tally to put up on the attendance board: "The number of disciples was increasing" (6:1). And as the Church grew internally, it also grew externally: the disciples "grew in numbers" (9:31). The early followers of Christ planned their work and worked their plan. Each church planted a church, "the churches . . . grew daily in numbers" (16:5).

Jesus still calls His Church to focus on external growth. He says, "Come, follow me, . . . and I will make you fishers of men" (Matt. 4:19). He said He would make His followers "fishers of men" not "fish." What is your emphasis? Are you making leaders of fishers or are you leading fish? He calls the church to operate at four important levels:

- *Level 1—individuals,* winning them to Christ
- *Level 2—leaders,* equipping them for ministry
- *Level 3—daughter churches,* planting new and healthy churches
- *Level 4—mother churches,* developing strong churches

When we succeed in these four levels, leadership is developed, seminaries and extension studies are filled with persons called to ministry, and churches and districts multiply.

OVERCOMING CHURCH PROBLEMS

Not every church problem results from the wrong choice of carpet in the nursery, the struggle to keep the board chairman's wife at the piano, or the mortgage payment on the Youth Center. Some church problems stem from laying the wrong foundation. There are at least three church problems that must be overcome, if the church is to impact the world: (1) building-centeredness, (2) pastor-centeredness, and (3) member-centeredness. For the most part, the church has historically risen to the occasion in dealing with these problems.

First, the church overcomes building-centeredness by going. That is, it makes an effort to keep from focusing merely on things within the church building. This tradition inherited from pre-Reformation days remains deeply rooted in the Protestant church. But many churches are seeing exceptional growth through their outreach ministries. They are determined to keep their church from being a parking lot.

During the first 300 years of the Church, Christians did not build a single church building,[1] and the gospel was proclaimed to the known world. Without a video projector, sound equipment, lighting, or even a fellowship hall, the first Christians made a spiritual impression on their entire world. How? They met people where they lived, worked, and gathered. One to one, in the home or in the marketplace, they shared the Good News.

It can still be done. We can do an extreme makeover of the church by tearing down the walls that keep the people with a *message* from the people who are in a *mess!* And in the process, we can save on the church's light bill. Meeting in homes, restaurants, or community centers not only saves electricity but also creates greater opportunity.

Certainly, the church building has an important place in the life of the church. But there will be no life in the church unless the church goes out once in a while.

For example, during the first 70 years, the Church of the Nazarene organized 349 churches in South America. Each year the South American church received enough money from foreign sources to build 5 churches, and that is all they built. Then, implementing the plan of each Christian reaching another person with the gospel, each pastor training another pastor, and each church planting another church (which did not depend on outside sources to succeed), in less than 10 years, 900 churches were organized. Breaking out of the confines of the church building resulted in breaking cultural barriers. The church went to the people, and in return, the people came to church.

Second, the church overcomes pastor-centeredness by recruiting. In most churches, the pastor does everything. His secret job description is to tarry, marry, bury, and carry. In between, he or she is expected to prepare a sermon fit for televising on all the major religious channels! Many times, the pastor does the ministry of the church single-handedly. The rest of the church cheers or jeers, puts a dollar in the offering plate to offset pastoral expenses, and waits for the next performance.

Where there has been the greatest growth in local churches, there has been the greatest recruitment of lay ministry teams, with the pastor assisting these teams in ministering. Here's an illustration of why it works: Suppose we had a bricklayer building a wall. If we wanted the wall built more effectively, and more rapidly, it would be necessary to buy more tools—more plumb lines, more buckets, and more shovels. But we'll also need more bricklayers. Churches that are pastor-centered have the tools for making an impact on their community, but they're only using one bricklayer.

Ephesians 4:11-12 suggests that there are other bricklayers available: "It was he who gave some to be apostles, some to be prophets, some to be evangelists, and some to be pastors and teachers, to prepare God's people for works of service, so that the body of Christ may be built up." The pastor-bricklayer's task is to recruit more pastor-bricklayers.

If the pastor wants to build the Kingdom, he or she must raise up leaders. In a recent message, Rev. Norman Shoemaker gave some excellent advice on this important issue. He said that there are five types of persons who need to be discipled. Here is a summary of what he shared:

1. The *curious* are those who attend church once in a while, send their children to the Sunday School, and look in occasionally to see what they are doing.
2. The *interested* are those that agree with the gospel but have not yet made a final decision to accept Christ.
3. *Converts* are those who have already accepted Christ but who haven't committed themselves to His service.
4. The *consecrated* are those who desire to become involved in Christian service.
5. *Leaders* are those who have already accepted a responsibility within the church—leaders in the young people's society, Sunday School, missionary society, and so on.

Which group has the greatest potential for leadership? The consecrated—those who are ready to commit themselves to the work of the Lord. Following the pattern of your denomination's pioneer leaders, they will be recruited, equipped, supported, and sent.

It is not difficult to discover within a group of 50 persons the curious, the interested, the converts, the consecrated, and the leaders. The consecrated are the reliable people of which the apostle speaks in 2 Tim. 2:2. What is the church to do with the rest? (1) Evangelize the curious; (2) engage the interested; and (3) disciple the converts, leading them to a life of holiness.

In one church, Sunday evening services had the largest attendance and were considered to be the most important services. Then its pastor received light on recruiting leaders. The pastor began meeting with *consecrated* members on Monday nights. Soon, that became the most important meeting of the week. The pastor determined that "spiritual milk" was adequate for Sunday night, but the Monday meeting called for strong spiritual meat.

Fifteen leaders started 5 prayer cells. They depended on the pastor to give them materials and instruction. Soon there were 10 prayer cells, and then 15 more. The church began to grow—from 40 in attendance to 290. Another Sunday night service was added.

Later, some of the prayer cells became missions. Then two missions became organized churches. One began with 70 members; the other with 35. The one with 35 members grew to 200 and opened 2 new churches. The person who became the pastor of a new church was one of those 15 original members of the Monday night meeting.

Today, the mother church has more than 500 members and continues to grow. Other churches of that city followed the same plan until there are now 17 churches. Plans are now being made for an evangelistic impact with a goal of organizing 20 new churches.

The district now has more than 1,000 members. Why? Simply put, the pastors are becoming more decentralized, and they are putting their energies into discipling leaders. They have learned that the task of the pastor is not to play all the instruments in the orchestra. Rather he or she is to conduct.

Third, the church overcomes member-centeredness by equipping. In member-centered churches, everything that is done is done for the church. Preaching, praying, singing, teaching, giving, and handshaking are all for the benefit of the church's members. Statistics covering 80 years tell us that 95 percent of believers have never won a single person to Christ! The Master said, "You are my friends if you do what I command you" (John 15:14). One of His commandments is to "take the church on the road"—to announce the good news of salvation and to make disciples.

THE POTENTIAL

Believers have an incredible potential, which can be developed. Without that development, church members soon excuse themselves from evangelism. Believing they don't have the training or the gifts, they expect the pastor to do the evangelism and discipling.

Without a single evangelism course, believers still have the means to impact their world—their home, neighborhood, community, or country. They have their personal testimony! The first evangelist in the New Testament was a homeless man who slept in a cemetery (see Mark 5). He was demon-possessed. They called him Legion. He was dirty and despairing. But after a four-hour meeting with the Master, his life was changed. He was forgiven, healed, cleansed, and sound of mind. That's a pretty tough secret to keep!

As Jesus was leaving, the Bible says, "The man from whom the demons had gone out begged to go with him" (Luke 8:38). Jesus gave him the command that is the same to every believer. "Return home and tell how much God has done for you" (v. 39).

What was the result? High impact! One man, touched by God, made a spiritual impression on the 10 cities of the Decapolis, "And all the people were amazed" (Mark 5:20). The strategies that we present in this book are tools that any believer can use for "high impact."

FOLLOW THE LEADERS

People in your church have the potential. The rest is up to you: recruiting, training, supporting, and sending. It is estimated that after five years, a faithful church member has listened to 800 sermons and sung 2,000 hymns and 1,500 choruses. What can we say about this member? He or she has unconverted loved ones and friends, a wide network of associates who need the gospel, and neighbors hungry for something that will give them hope. But he or she is also a potential soul winner, potential cell group leader, potential evangelistic crusade coordinator, and potential pastor. This person is the hope for aggressive church multiplication.

In addition to being the most effective channel for bringing the lost to Christ, people recruited and trained to reach the lost also have the potential to reach great numbers of people. For example, if 100 Big Brothers and Big Sisters (we'll learn about this later) were to be enlisted from a church of 200 members, they would be praying for 1,000 persons who do not know Christ. In one campaign there were 80 Big Brothers praying for and inviting 800 unchurched people. In three days of evangelistic services, over 300 people who had never been to an evangelical church accepted Christ.

Such outreach all starts at the desk in the desert—learning with Moses how to maximize ministry without minimizing strength. It continues with Paul—recruiting and training people like Timothy and Titus. It is in sync with the heartbeat of a denomination's leaders—people who know firsthand the impact a dedicated people can make on a region or an entire country.

Follow the leaders. If you're going to be a part of a movement that will impact your world, unleash the potential that is in the members of the church. The biblical and practical strategies presented in this book are designed to help you do this.

In the next section, we will take a closer look at the strategy of Jesus, who as we observed earlier was and is the unmatched Leader of leaders.

③ THE JESUS STRATEGY

The life and ministry of Jesus of Nazareth not only changed lives but also changed the course of history. His leadership was integral to that influence. He formed a small group of undeveloped unknowns into a formidable force—a 12-soldier, weaponless army that made political and religious kingdoms tremble; a 12-man committee that brought more healing and help to masses of people than any other organization in history.

By following the leadership model of Jesus, the 12 disciples became leaders themselves. As Jesus had gathered them, they gathered others. As He had poured His life into them, they poured their lives into others. As they had been trained, they trained. As they had been encouraged, they encouraged. As they had been built into a leadership team, they developed a core of leaders. With Jesus' example fresh in their hearts and minds and with the empowerment of a risen Christ, they built churches out of cell groups and religious movements out of churches—all of which still influences our society.

Everything they did was an extension of what Jesus had done. From small-group meetings to citywide campaigns, they followed the Jesus strategy. In this chapter and the next we will present this strategy as another important part of the philosophy that resulted in aggressive church multiplication and discipleship. Jesus' mandate for discipling others—the Great Commission—encapsulates this: "Then Jesus came to them and said, 'All authority in heaven and on earth has been given to me. Therefore go and make disciples of all nations, baptizing them in the name of the Father and of the Son and of the Holy Spirit, and teaching them to obey everything I have commanded you. And surely I will be with you always, to the very end of the age'" (Matt. 28:18-20).

Yet Jesus not only commanded discipleship but also practiced it. In just 36 months, He turned a group of unlearned men into unequaled leaders who impacted the entire world. We can gain much by studying and using the same 10-step discipleship process He used.

1. JESUS DEPENDED ON HIS FATHER (JOHN 12:49)

After laying aside the power and authority He had in heaven, Jesus depended on His Heavenly Father for His life and ministry on earth. He says in John 12:49, "I did not speak of my own accord, but the Father who sent me commanded me what to say and how to say it."

Jesus began and ended His earthly ministry by praying to His Father. From the beginning of His public ministry, fasting and praying 40 days in the wilderness (Matt. 4), to the last hours before His crucifixion (Luke 22:42), Jesus relied on His relationship with His Father.

During His last staff meeting, Jesus reflected on that relationship in a prayer for His disciples (John 17:1-21). That model prayer revealed much about His leadership strategy:

First, it reaffirmed His ministry purpose and the resource for that ministry.

After Jesus said this, he looked toward heaven and prayed: "Father, the time has come. Glorify your Son, that your Son may glorify you. For you granted him authority over all people that he might give eternal life to all those you have given him. Now this is eternal life: that they may know you, the only true God, and Jesus Christ, whom you have sent. I have brought you glory on earth by completing the work you gave me to do. And now, Father, glorify me in your presence with the glory I had with you before the world began" *(vv. 1-5).*

Second, it communicated His intent to continue His work on earth through the lives of the disciples.

I have revealed you to those whom you gave me out of the world. They were yours; you gave them to me and they have obeyed your word. Now they know that everything you have given me comes from you. For I gave them the words you gave me and they accepted them. They knew with certainty that I came from you, and they believed that you sent me. I pray for them. I am not praying for the world, but for those you have given me, for they are yours. All I have is yours, and all you have is mine. And glory has come to me through them. I will remain in the world no longer, but they are still in the world, and I am coming to you. Holy Father, protect them by the power of your name—the name you gave me—so that they may be one as we are one. While I was with them, I protected them and kept them safe by that name you gave me. None has been lost except the one doomed to destruction so that Scripture would be fulfilled *(vv. 6-12).*

Third, it encouraged and directed His disciples.

I am coming to you now, but I say these things while I am still in the world, so that they may have the full measure of my joy within them. I have given them your word and the world has hated them, for they are not of the world any more than I am of the world. My prayer is not that you take them out of the world but that you protect them from the evil one. They are not of the world, even as I am not of it. Sanctify them by the truth; your word is truth. As you sent me into the world, I have sent them into the world. For them I sanctify myself, that they too may be truly sanctified" *(vv. 13-19).*

Fourth, it revealed His strategy for world evangelization by the multiplication of disciples.

My prayer is not for them alone. I pray also for those who will believe in me through their message, that all of them may be one, Father, just as you are in me and I am in you. May they also be in us so that the world may believe that you have sent me *(vv. 20-21).*

In the very same way, every Christian leader needs not only a plan but also a power source! Nothing of any long-term effect will happen without God's direction or intervention. As Jesus says in John 15:5, "I am the vine; you are the branches. If a man remains in me and I in him, he will bear much fruit; apart from me you can do nothing."

2. JESUS HAD AN EVANGELISTIC PURPOSE (LUKE 19:10)

While on earth, Jesus did many things. *But He was always focused on the main thing.* He had a clear objective, which He communicated to Zacchaeus during their life-changing meeting: "Jesus said to him, 'Today salvation has come to this house. . . . For the Son of Man came to seek and to save what was lost'" (Luke 19:9-10).

He never got off track. He refused to be sidelined by the things that did not contribute to the main objective—redemption. Jesus knew He had only three years to fulfill His earthly ministry. So His main concern was to coordinate His efforts—to train those who would continue to announce the gospel. It is a wise lesson for every Christian leader. Refuse to be sidetracked. Focus on your focus. Remember, if everything is important, then nothing is! World evangelization requires organizational structure. But structure isn't more important than salvation. World evangelization needs a coordinated effort. But the most important teamwork is between the leader and his or her Lord. Every act of organizational service is about souls!

3. JESUS WISELY SELECTED HIS DISCIPLES (MATT. 10)

It's significant that Jesus didn't choose His team from the Ivy League of His day. He went to the boat docks and found fishermen such as Peter, James, and John. He stopped at the corporate headquarters and went back to the accounting office to call Matthew the tax collector. He found workers and put them to a greater work.

He carefully chose them. In the Bible, men and women who were used by God were workers. Many were even called during their working hours. This was the case with Moses, Gideon, Elisha, David, and Samuel.

The call of King David is a great example. Guided by the voice of God, Samuel went to the house of Jesse to anoint one of his sons as king. Seven of the sons filled out applications. But the prophet asked, "Are these all the sons you have?" Jesse responded, "There is still the youngest, . . . but he is tending the sheep" (1 Sam. 16:11).

David was in the field with a shepherd's staff in his hands while his brothers were in the house being fitted for crowns. But the crowns wouldn't fit. Their heads were too big! God needed a servant not a star. He needed someone whose skills could be molded, someone who had a heart for God, not glory. Samuel commanded them to bring the eight-year-old from the field. God had made the final choice. When God's prophet placed his hands on David's head, the Spirit of the Lord came upon him (v. 13).

As we select leaders, we should be equally as careful to pick people who are workers. The Lord isn't looking for people who have nothing to do. In Jesus' early years of ministry the people said, "Isn't this the carpenter? Isn't this Mary's son?" (Mark 6:3). Jesus was known as a worker before He was known as a teacher. We must select people who are workers.

4. HE MOTIVATED HIS DISCIPLES (LUKE 10:22-24)

After selecting His team, the Lord motivated them. How? By taking a personal interest in them. He says in Luke 10:22-24:

> "All things have been committed to me by my Father. No one knows who the Son is except the Father, and no one knows who the Father is except the Son and those to whom the Son chooses to reveal him." Then he turned to his disciples and said privately, "Blessed are the eyes that see what you see. For I tell you that many prophets and kings wanted to see what you see but did not see it, and to hear what you hear but did not hear it."

Jesus was both a prophet and a king, but He chose to privately share the secrets of the heavens with commoners.

Jesus also spent extended periods of time with His disciples trying to motivate them by example. They were high on His list of priorities. For example, He once excused himself from an audience of 4,000 persons to take a boat ride with them (Mark 8:10). The time that Jesus spent with the multitudes was limited. However, He spent 1,000 days with His disciples. Mark 6:1 recounts, "Jesus left there and went to his hometown, accompanied by his disciples."

Authority and respect are earned. They aren't legislated. They're born in times of sharing and in times of giving in the interest of another. The disciples were motivated to care about the needs of others by the personal interest Jesus showed in them.

5. HE INSTRUCTED HIS TEAM (MATT. 10:5—11:1)

In the last 37 verses of Matt. 10, we find 75 instructions that the Lord Jesus gave to His disciples. He told them what they had to do (vv. 5-8), what they should not do (vv. 9-10), and what they could expect (v. 10). He gave them the information they needed (v. 11) and told them where they should stay (vv. 11-12) and how to respond if they were not received (vv. 13-15).

Who should give instructions to the ministry team? Clearly it should be the ministry team leader. Just as an officer gives instructions to his or her soldiers and a father gives instructions to his children, the Christian leader is responsible to give instructions to the team. A leader must lead.

6. HE GAVE RESPONSIBILITY TO HIS TEAM (MATT. 21:6)

Jesus gave His disciples not only instructions but also responsibility. Jesus was the master coach. He knew His team couldn't spend all of their time in the locker room or on the bench. They needed to be on the field putting the things they had learned into practice. Matt. 21:6 says, "The disciples went and did as Jesus had instructed them."

Did some of the team make mistakes? Absolutely! You remember the apostle Peter? But mistakes or not, the team needed the responsibility of playing time. The coach stays on the sidelines. Players make the plays.

Workers need more than recruitment, training, or motivation. They need to work! They need to practice their principles. The strategy for aggressive church multiplication begins with aggressive discipleship.

7. HE GAVE THEM AUTHORITY (LUKE 9:1)

Along with responsibility, Jesus gave His disciples authority. He gave them credentials to enter the stronghold of the enemy as ambassadors of the King of Kings. Luke 9:1 says, "When Jesus had called the Twelve together, he gave them power and authority to drive out all demons and to cure diseases."

We can picture their victory march. We can see Satan looking at the disciples after the Lord had given them authority. To his horror, he hears them saying, "In the name of Jesus . . ." and watches as the demon-possessed are set free. "In the name of Jesus . . ." again echoes across the battlefield. Lepers are cleansed and the sick are healed. And to add insult to Satan's injury, the disciples announce that the kingdom of heaven has come.

After many accepted the message, Satan must have thought, *I knew that Jesus had authority, but these fishermen and tax collectors are doing miracles too. This is getting out of hand!*

When Jesus saw it, He became a color commentator similar to those in the broadcaster booth of a football game: "I saw Satan fall like lightning from heaven" (Luke 10:18). Why did He say that Satan had fallen? Because the disciples had received power and authority over him.

When modern-day disciples have the responsibility *and* authority to represent their church on the field, it is the beginning of a movement. But watch the sequence: Jesus got His authority from His Heavenly Father. The disciples had authority because they were subject to Jesus. When will Christian leaders have their authority? When they are subject to authority. When we are subject to our immediate supervisors in the church, we share their authority. Submission has a payoff. James the apostle said, "God opposes the proud but gives grace to the humble" (James 4:6).

Conversely, when leaders put their *position* on parade they lose authority. The Lord Jesus led with humility, and He taught humility to His disciples. That is why they had authority. They were subject to the Master. Let us submit ourselves in order to have authority.

8. HE PERIODICALLY EVALUATED THE WORK (LUKE 10:17)

Kingdom efforts need quality control. Even at the Creation, there was an evaluation: "God saw all that he had made, and it was very good" (Gen. 1:31). Jesus carried out the company policy. He gave His disciples a 40-day assignment. When they returned, they gave an account of their work. The report was good: "The seventy-two returned with joy and said, 'Lord, even the demons submit to us in your name'" (Luke 10:17). The Lord used the quality control time to motivate them even further: "Rejoice that your names are written in heaven" (v. 20).

If the corporate world can use performance standards to evaluate their influence, so can the Church. Goal setting, for instance, is useless without a periodic check to see if goals are being reached. As another example, if a community or region is the target of an evangelistic campaign, the leadership should keep tabs on the progress. The evaluation often reveals necessary adjustments—more workers, different timeframe, new approaches, additional assignments, and so on.

9. HE CLEARLY ARTICULATED THE MISSION (MATT. 28:19-20)

"Therefore go and make disciples of all nations, baptizing them in the name of the Father and of the Son and of the Holy Spirit, and teaching them to obey everything I have commanded you. And surely I am with you always, to the very end of the age" (Matt. 28:19-20).

As we have observed, this is the Jesus strategy. When the church puts it into practice, it ceases to be an organization and becomes a living organism that reproduces itself. The organization, although good, is only the means to fulfill the mission. The sequence is important:

GO: This is the imperative action.
MAKE: This is the task.
DISCIPLES: This is the objective.
ALL NATIONS: This is the place.
TEACHING THEM: This is the doctrine.

We must make the mission clear. We can't assume that our team understands the objective. There may be those who have spent their entire life in church circles and still do not understand that world evangelization is the bottom line of Christianity. A Christian is a "Christ one." The Church is ultimately called to make Christ ones out of every person on the planet.

Isn't that a tall request? Absolutely! But the command isn't greater than the Commander. He lived sinless on the earth, died on the Cross, and then left an empty tomb as a warning to the devil and his angels. That is the Christ who promised to walk beside the Church as it marches into battle!

10. HE ENABLED THE TEAM (LUKE 24:49)

In Luke 24:49 Jesus said, "I am going to send you what my Father has promised; but stay in the city until you have been clothed with power from on high." This promise of the ages was fulfilled in a moment:

> When the day of Pentecost came, they were all together in one place. Suddenly a sound like the blowing of a violent wind came from heaven and filled the whole house where they were sitting. They saw what seemed to be tongues of fire that separated and came to rest on each of them. All of them were filled with the Holy Spirit and began to speak in other tongues as the Spirit enabled them *(Acts 2:1-4)*.

Notice, how "the Spirit enabled them." In one glorious moment, the cowering were transformed into the courageous. Their prayer for power was answered!

Before Pentecost, the disciples were fearful. Following the Crucifixion, a woman said to a disciple loitering near the fire where Jesus' death was being discussed, "You are one of them." Peter said, "No, I am not." Two others at the campfire made the same accusation. Terrified by the association, Peter denied that he knew the Master. He had experienced the nine steps that we have mentioned: he learned to pray, he had a strategy, he was chosen, he was motivated, he had instructions, he was given responsibility, he had authority, he was evaluated, and he had been commanded to fulfill the gospel mission. However, he did not have the promised power.

After Pentecost, the same disciple courageously stood before thousands and leveled an accusation of his own: "You killed the author of life" (Acts 3:15). Now he was ready to die for Christ. Why? He had been enabled. He was empowered by the Holy Spirit.

Before Pentecost the disciples lacked power. They were like a vehicle with a good engine, good tires, and a good paint job but with an empty gas tank.

When the Holy Spirit came upon them, they went out to revolutionize the world. Within their lifetime the known world had heard of Jesus. God had enabled them to fulfill the mission of world evangelization by filling them with His Spirit.

In the chapters that follow we will take a look at the Big Brothers and Big Sisters plan, which we mentioned earlier; it is based on the model Jesus gave us. We will also explore the use of prayer cells, which provide homes where the converted and the discipled can learn and grow. But first let's look at how to use the Each One Win One plan in aggressive outreach.

II.
PREPARATION

④ EACH ONE WIN ONE

Evangelism is not accidental. It happens on purpose. We explained the importance of an *external* leadership that will mobilize believers. Now let's explore methods for mobilizing. We begin with the program Each One Win One.

Barna Research Group says, "The unchurched are sophisticated enough, and varied enough, that it will take a plan for reaching them. While many churches have attempted to simply be themselves and hope that the unchurched will visit and decide to stay, it will take more than naive hope and laudable desires to attract and retain the unchurched."[1]

Jesus Bernat, a district leader in Uruguay, once said to a visiting denominational leader, "We know that someday you will leave, but I want to tell you that what you have taught us, and what we have learned about the system of growth in the church, will never die."

When one person catches the vision for sharing Christ—and learns how to do it—it will affect everyone around that person. We believe that evangelism sparks can result in a raging evangelistic fire. Rev. Bernat used the Each One Win One system of evangelism to take a district that had been labeled a place where the church could not grow to a place of phenomenal growth. At his fifth district assembly, he reported 19 newly organized churches and 730 new members. In his sixth district assembly, he reported 16 more organized churches and a gain of 728 new members.

The Holy Spirit wants to help us build the Church everywhere. And He wants to use *your* church in the process! Think of the blessing it would be to impact your community by winning many people to Christ! Think of the thrill of sending trained laypersons from your church to start new churches! In the following pages, we will show you how that can become a reality.

THE PURPOSE

Each One Win One is based on the biblical principle that every believer is called to advance the kingdom of God. Prior to His ascension, Jesus gathered His followers in the Upper Room. There, He explained His part in the personal fulfillment of Old Testament prophecy. But He also explained that the disciples had a part, as well. Luke 24:45-49 says:

> He opened their minds so they could understand the Scriptures. He told them, "This is what is written: The Christ will suffer and rise from the dead on the third day, and repentance and forgiveness of sins will be preached in his name to all nations, beginning at Jerusalem. You are witnesses of these things. I am going to send you what my Father has promised; but stay in the city until you have been clothed with power from on high."

After Pentecost, witnessing became the norm. Focusing on building the Kingdom, the Spirit-filled believers were on a mission. We believe that this mission wasn't the property of first-century Christians; it belongs to every believer. Every follower of Jesus Christ has a calling to win *others* to Christ.

Each One Win One assumes that *every believer* is a part of that plan and can impact his or her world to build the kingdom of Christ on the earth. Its purpose is to encourage them to accept that responsibility and to be accountable for their personal mission.

PREPARING THE CHURCH THROUGH PRAYER

Every local church has its own personality. There are many evangelistic strategies, and not every strategy is a good fit. But the Each One Win One plan is one that has been used by a wide number of churches, with great success. It begins with the pastor. The church's leader must lay a Spirit-led foundation for the presentation. A series of messages on the church, spiritual gifts, stewardship, soul winners in the Bible, salvation, or sanctification may be used in preparing for the launch of the strategy. Bulletin inserts, newsletter articles, PowerPoint presentations, skits, and so on, may supplement the sermon series. The intent of the preparation time is to create an awareness of the spiritual needs of the community, and the believer's responsibility to meet those needs.

Prayer chains, prayer meetings, and prayer and fasting should be utilized weeks ahead of the church's Each One Win One launch. From a list of prayer requests, the local church can begin to trust God for an outpouring of His Spirit in the lives of the church members, loved ones and friends, and the surrounding neighborhoods of the church.

THE DEDICATION SERVICE

The Each One Win One program is launched with a service of dedication. Working with the worship leader and the musicians, the pastor will want to create an atmosphere of praise to Christ for His sacrifice and lead the people in consecrating their lives to the Savior as an offering of thanksgiving.

The pastor's message may be based on one of several passages that emphasize soul winning: Matt. 5:15; Matt. 10:32; Matt. 28:19-20; Mark 4:21; Mark 5:19; Luke 4:18-19; Luke 8; Luke 12:8-9; John 4:28-42; John 8:32; John 15; Acts 1:8; Acts 4:18-20; Acts 5:20; Acts 10:36; Acts 20:24; Rom. 1:16; Rom. 10; Rom. 16:25-26; 1 Cor. 9:16-18; 2 Cor. 4:13-14; Eph. 3:8-11; Eph. 6:15-20; Phil. 3:7-14; 1 Tim. 6:12-13; 2 Tim. 1:8; Heb. 2; 1 Pet. 3:15; Rev. 12:11.

The purpose of the message is to create enthusiasm and encourage the people to make a total commitment. The pastor should explain the program Each One Win One with as much detail as possible and in an inspiring way. He or she should explain how more persons can be won to Christ and what the responsibility of the church is for each person who is won.

At the conclusion of the sermon, there will be a moment of dedication. The pastor or leader will then invite volunteers to come forward. In response to the call for commitment, they will sign their names in the left-hand column of an Each One Win One poster, promising that with the help of God, they will

1. Try to win one person to Christ during the year
2. Pray that God will help them win that new person to Christ
3. List persons for whom they will be praying
4. Disciple the new Christian by
    a. Teaching him or her a basic course for new Christians and helping the person to be faithful to God
    b. Teaching the person to tithe

c. Teaching the person to be faithful to the church by participating in its services and activities

d. Helping the person to seek the infilling of the Holy Spirit

e. Preparing the person for baptism

f. Encouraging the person to attend a membership class

g. Standing by the person's side on the day he or she is received into membership

h. Teaching the person to be a soul winner

There will be those who come to the church and accept Christ even though they were not invited by one of the members. The pastor or leader should assign the new converts to someone in the church who will be responsible for their individual growth.

THE FOLLOW-UP

The Each One Win One plan should be promoted every week following the launch:

1. Share how it is working in the church. (Take advantage of the success of some of your members! Ask the workers to testify how God is helping them in the plan of Each One Win One.)

2. Introduce new converts to the congregation to tell what God has done in their lives. Have the converts testify about how thankful they are that someone took an interest in them, guided them to Christ, and helped them become members of the church.

3. Prepare a certificate of recognition listing the name of the person who has won someone to Christ (see Appendix M). The presentation may be made during a worship service or in a fellowship meeting.

4. Schedule prayer meetings. It is important to constantly emphasize prayer, not only for the converts but also for the workers. Assign or ask members to be special intercessors who will pray that God will help the persons involved in the Each One Win One plan.

Anything that creates enthusiasm and incentive for the members of the church will help to sustain and give new life to the local church effort.

DRAWING THE NET: RECEIVING NEW MEMBERS

Some pastors wait several months to receive new members into the church—until they have a *group* of persons. It is better to receive members each month, making it a special occasion for the church and for the new members. If a pastor is constantly emphasizing the receiving of new members, the congregation will see the importance of membership and will help others become a part of the church. There are other benefits in regularly receiving new members:

1. It creates enthusiasm in the local church.

2. It creates an atmosphere of victory.

3. It motivates.

4. It sets goals.

5. It helps the church fulfill the Great Commission.

6. It stimulates growth and the outreach of the local church.

If the pastor sets a fixed monthly date for the reception of members, the church can work toward a new-member goal. Often it is more by accident than by planning that a church receives members. Congregations are often like a football team playing a goalless game, running all over the playing field but never crossing a goal line. For football teams—and churches—having a set goal to head toward is best.

The reception of members can be a wonderful time for the church and a special part of the Each One Win One plan. The service in which members are received needs to be well planned and well promoted. It ought to be a very special service, with a message that emphasizes the importance of church membership and gives information about the process of becoming a member. The membership service also should emphasize how the Each One Win One plan works.

The pastor should prepare new converts for church membership by taking two important steps. First, he or she should make sure that a current member (mentor) is responsible for each convert in the Each One Win One plan and that the mentoring members have the training and tools they need to disciple new converts. (One important tool is the *Basic Bible Studies* lessons developed by Chic Shaver for new converts, which can be ordered from Beacon Hill Press of Kansas City, www.beaconhillbooks.com.)

Second, the pastor should see that membership classes are available. He or she may prefer to teach the classes. Their length and time may vary, but the classes should be well organized and well promoted.

At the service where members are received into the church, some important elements should be included:

1. The pastor should invite the new converts to come forward with the person who has won them to the Lord or with the mentor who will be responsible for them.

2. The pastor should share how God has specifically blessed each new convert and should mention something of special interest about each one. He or she should also tell how God has blessed the one who was responsible for winning and/or mentoring them.

3. The pastor may ask for a testimony from each new member and a testimony from the person who was responsible for them.

4. After the pastor has received the new member into the church, the Each One Win One plan should be explained, and the pastor should ask each of the converts to sign the poster in the right-hand column (designed by the local church), opposite the name of the one that led them to Christ. (Note: If a person has won more than one convert, he or she should sign in a special space provided, and the new converts will sign their names opposite the soul winner's name.)

5. The pastor should then invite each new convert to sign on one of the spaces in the left-hand column of the Each One Win One poster. Signing in that column signifies that with the help of the Lord, the convert will also be responsible to win a new person to Christ.

6. The pastor should invite the persons who have been responsible for the new converts to sign their names again at the end of the list indicating that with the help of the Lord, they will try to win *another* person for Christ during the year.

OVERCOMING EVANGELISM BARRIERS

Christian leaders should not be discouraged if the initial reaction to the plan is less than enthusiastic. There are several barriers that stand in the way.

The devil is the first barrier to evangelism. The enemy of the Church hates it when believers are unified in any cause—let alone the cause of tearing down hell's strongholds and introducing people to Christ. John 10:10 makes this clear: "The thief comes only to steal and kill and destroy." Be prepared (1 Pet. 5:8). The enemy *will* try to shatter your plans. He will do it in devious ways. He will urge procrastination, cause dissension, and sow confusion. He will do his best to sidetrack the church when it commits to reaching people for Christ.

The devil's roadblocks are no match for prayer, however. A concert of prayer, a night of prayer, days of fasting and prayer, prayer chains, and other scheduled prayer times are effective weapons against the enemy's attacks. Don't forget the battle call: "The weapons we fight with are not the weapons of the world. On the contrary, they have divine power to demolish strongholds" (2 Cor. 10:4).

Tradition is the second barrier to evangelism. Tragically, the church has become accustomed to paying its staff to do its ministry. Making the leap over the attitudes of died-in-the-wool pew sitters will not be easily accomplished. But it can be done. This is a marketing age. The people who listen to the pastor's weekly commercials are used to hearing the real ones offered by the media. They are used to being motivated by what they are told will benefit them. The leader's task is to motivate them for what will genuinely benefit them. Various means can help accomplish this, such as the testimonies of satisfied customers. Christian films, lay witness teams, and missions conferences can add power to your mission. The church has never had as many resources available as it has today. Utilize them.

Disorganization is the third barrier to evangelism. It's not true that everybody loves surprises. Spur-of-the-moment plans—evangelistic or otherwise—can cause more pain than pleasure to a congregation. People in the pew need leadership—Spirit-filled leadership, trained leadership. They need to know that someone has put careful thought into the program that will call for their time, their talent, or their treasure. A carefully written, carefully presented plan is essential to the congregation's buying-in.

Insincerity is the fourth barrier to evangelism. A leader calling troops into battle who has never been to war will likely find it difficult to sound the battle cry. A leader leads by example. Someone who is not personally committed to soul winning will have a tough time convincing others of its necessity. The apostle Paul gave a challenging invitation to those whom he led: "Follow my example, as I follow the example of Christ" (1 Cor. 11:1). As the old adage suggests, "Evangelism is better caught than taught."

The experience of seeing someone lead another to Christ is life-changing! Someone who has witnessed the conversion of a lost man, woman, boy, or girl could very well be the next leader in the church who will inspire "each one to win one."

Fear is the fifth barrier to evangelism. One of the main reasons many Christians do not share their faith is fear. We encounter all kinds of fears. The fear of the unknown, the fear of rejection, the fear of speaking in public, and the fear of ostracism are all realities in the church. There is almost an evangelism phobia looming in churches.

The evangelism leader has an opportunity to fight the phobia. First, people must know about the *promise.* With His last words, Jesus sent us to be witnesses by His power and authority: "You will receive power . . . and you will be my witnesses" (Acts 1:8).

Second, people must know that witnessing isn't an option:

> You did not choose me, but I chose you and appointed you to go and bear fruit—fruit that will last. Then the Father will give you whatever you ask in my name. This is my command: Love each other. If the world hates you, keep in mind that it hated me first. If you belonged to the world, it would love you as its own. As it is, you do not belong to the world, but I have chosen you out of the world *(John 15:16-19).*

Third, people must know they will *get* more out of witnessing than they will *give:* "He who goes out weeping, carrying seed to sow, will return with songs of joy, carrying sheaves with him" (Ps. 126:6). There aren't many sad soul winners. The thrill of victory is the result of leading another person to Christ. Soul winning is that "something missing" in most churches. And it's a great antidote to evangelism phobia.

Inferiority is the sixth evangelism barrier to evangelism. Twenty-first-century Christians live in a world where faith is mocked and foolishness is magnified. To go into the world means abandoning one's comfort zone. The church suffers from and expresses its feelings of inferiority: "We can't possibly match the world's entertainment." "We don't have the means that others have." "We'll be laughed at."

The church needs to be reminded that it's on the *winning side.* Its Captain won the war! Calvary put an end to the boasts of the devil and his followers. John shouted it from the pages of Scripture, "You, dear children, are from God and have overcome them, because the one who is in you is greater than the one who is in the world" (1 John 4:4).

The church emphasizes that believers need to be prepared in scriptural knowledge to win others for Christ. But believers do not require a lot of preparation to testify about what God has done in their personal lives. Personal evangelism is a marvelous method that God has used to make the church grow. Though every believer may not have the gift of evangelism, he or she has the gift of salvation. And salvation's gift isn't something a person can effectively keep quiet about!

The Each One Win One plan is a wonderful way to break the silence. It gives a powerful voice to the church. It is a voice of joy over the forgiveness of sins—a voice of victory for what Christ has done and what He has promised.

In our next chapter we will guide you to another effective strategy for reaching the unchurched in your community and impacting your world for Christ—the Big Brothers and Big Sisters plan.

III.

DISCIPLESHIP

⑤ THE BIG BROTHERS AND BIG SISTERS MODEL

The Each One Win One plan is a basic tool for helping believers participate in our call to win the world to Christ. The Big Brothers and Big Sisters[1] plan is an additional—and effective—system for evangelism and discipleship that may be an even better fit for your church's ministry.

We present the two programs separately because we want to encourage the church to use all of its gifts and abilities to win others for Christ. It can be presented at any time after the dedication service for Each One Win One.

All too often when someone is won to the Lord, he or she does not receive adequate follow-up and is lost. With the Big Brothers and Big Sisters plan, we are not only involving the "90 and 5" (the 95 percent of all Christians who have never led someone to Christ) but also enabling them to disciple new believers.

PRESENTATION OF THE BIG BROTHERS AND BIG SISTERS MODEL

Like Each One Win One, the Big Brothers and Big Sisters plan begins with a service of dedication—including an informative and enthusiastic sermon—and is followed by an opportunity for responders to be consecrated as Big Brothers or Big Sisters, or a service of consecration. There are three basic steps in the plan: (1) Praying for 10 unsaved friends over a two-month period, (2) inviting and bringing those for whom they have prayed to an evangelistic campaign, and (3) discipling those who accept Christ as a result (perhaps over several years). (See Appendixes E and J.)

It is recommended that the consecration service be held two or three months before an evangelistic campaign. An outline for the presentation of the Big Brothers and Big Sisters plan is offered below. The pastor may adapt it for his or her situation.

The Big Brothers and Big Sisters Plan
(Sermon Outline and Presentation)

Bible reading: Acts 9:1-19

Introduction: "This is a night of consecration."

I. The Example of a Big Brother
   A. Jesus encounters Saul on the road to Damascus (vv. 3-7).
   B. Jesus speaks to Ananias in a vision (vv. 10-16).
      1. Jesus called them both by name. (The Lord is interested in everyone and knows everyone's name. Big Brothers and Big Sisters will have the names of 10 unconverted persons for whom they will be praying. God already knows them.)
      2. The Lord gave Saul's decision card to Ananias.
      3. Ananias was afraid. (Explain the story, applying it to the fear of presenting the gospel.)

C. Ananias met Saul where he was (vv. 17-18).
   1. Ananias went to Saul's house.
   2. Ananias laid hands on Saul.
   3. Ananias explained his mission. He told Saul the Lord "has sent me."
      a. That Saul might see (a sign that the conversion had lasted three days).
      b. That Saul might be filled with the Holy Spirit (he was converted when he met Jesus).
      c. Saul was baptized (the external sign of his conversion).
      d. Saul stayed with the disciples (receiving basic discipleship).

II. Questions About the Big Brothers and Big Sisters Plan
   A. Who are Big Brothers and Big Sisters?
      1. Someone who has Christ in his or her heart.
      2. Someone who is a member of the local church.
      3. Someone who desires to win others to Christ.
      4. It may be someone who has never won another person to Christ and doesn't even know how. This is his or her opportunity.
   B. Why do we call them Big Brothers and Big Sisters?
      1. The name suggests that we should care for younger brothers and sisters.
      2. We are all equal before God. God does not have grandchildren.
      3. We become children of God through faith in Christ.
      4. Big Brothers and Big Sisters is not a title; it is a commitment to care for others who need spiritual help.
      5. Those who receive Christ are brothers and sisters whom the family of God has been expecting.
   C. How do we become Big Brothers and Big Sisters?
      1. In the human family, a little brother or sister is born.
      2. In the church, there is a new birth.
      3. We should always anticipate the arrival of new brothers and sisters.
      4. We should list the names of 10 people who are unconverted: neighbors, friends, family members, and so on.
      5. Big Brothers and Big Sisters teams produce enthusiasm in the local church.
   D. When do we begin to be Big Brothers and Big Sisters?
      1. Right now! (Within two months a little brother or sister will be born.)
      2. We begin aiming toward a goal. We begin asking God, "Give me a little brother or sister. Help me to expect him or her."
      3. It is the responsibility of Big Brothers and Big Sisters to care for younger brothers and sisters—not the pastor.
      4. Pray each day for your brother or sister. Love the unconverted as God loves the world (John 3:16).
      5. Plan to visit your little brother or sister. You can say, "I have been praying for you every day for two months."
   E. What are the responsibilities of Big Brothers and Big Sisters?
      1. To consecrate themselves as Big Brothers and Big Sisters today.
      2. To prepare themselves mentally and spiritually through discipleship classes.
      3. To win others to Christ.

4. To disciple those who receive Christ. Big Brothers and Big Sisters will receive a decision card from the pastor, representing a new believer. (This decision card will be a duplicate; the original is in heaven. Jesus has already written the new convert's name in His Book of Life.)

III. Conclusion

    A. The Big Brothers and Big Sisters plan is a biblical plan.

    B. First, we must be spiritually prepared. We cannot give water if our container is empty.

    C. Each time God uses someone, it requires his or her consecration.

    D. When you meet your little brother or sister, you will remember this day of consecration.

    E. Jesus gave us an example by fasting and praying 40 days before He selected His first disciples.

    F. We will pray every day for 60 days, until God gives us a little brother or sister in the faith.

    G. We are expecting a great campaign and an abundant harvest. This is our hour of opportunity.

    H. We are in a battle, but "not against flesh and blood" (Eph. 6:12).

    I. We are part of a bigger plan in this campaign:

        1. The center for evangelism is the local church.

        2. Our enthusiasm could influence the entire denomination.

        3. Big Brothers and Big Sisters are the key.

The Invitation

    A. Invite all who will respond "Here am I" to the call of God: to stand.

    B. Ask them to come forward.

    C. Pray, consecrating them Big Brothers and Big Sisters.

THE BIG BROTHERS AND BIG SISTERS MEETING

Plan to have a meeting immediately following the service with those who have committed themselves as Big Brothers and Big Sisters. The leader must explain clearly what is involved in the plan. This is very important in selling the program.

1. Begin with prayer, thanking God for what He has done in the lives of those who have responded. Ask the responders each to take a Big Brothers and Big Sisters form and to mark the corresponding square, showing as day one the day they consecrated themselves as Big Brothers and Big Sisters.

2. Read 2 Tim. 2:2.

3. Ask each person to think of 10 persons for whom he or she will be praying and to write their names on the form provided within 24 hours (see Appendix J). (Clarify that these persons can be family members, neighbors, colleagues, or acquaintances; however, they must live in the city so they can be invited to an evangelistic campaign that will be held in two months.)

4. Explain what Big Brothers and Big Sisters are to do *before* the campaign.

    a. They are to pray each day (by name) for the salvation of the persons they have chosen as younger brothers and sisters, marking the square with an *X* that corresponds to the date when they have fulfilled their commitment for that day. (Tell them they will be knocking on the door of heaven 60 days before they will actually knock on the door of the person for whom they are praying to invite him or her to the evangelistic campaign. Also remind them that Jesus is interceding with them for those 10 persons [see Heb. 7:22-25].)

    b. They are to become accountable daily by marking an *X* in the column labeled "Prayed," following the name of the person for whom they have prayed. (Assure them that they—along with Jesus—have knocked on the Heavenly Father's door and that He will respond.)

    c. Following the 60 days of prayer, they will visit the 10 persons on their list and invite them to the evangelistic campaign. (Tell them to mark an *X* in the corresponding column after the name of the person whom they have invited to the campaign.)

5. Explain the work of Big Brothers and Big Sisters *during* the campaign.

    a. They are to mark an *X* in the corresponding column when a person whom they have invited attends the evangelistic campaign.

    b. They are to encourage their younger brothers and sisters to decide for Christ during the evangelistic meeting.

    c. They are to mark an *X* in the corresponding column for each person to identify all who receive Christ as their Savior.

6. Explain the work of Big Brothers and Big Sisters *following* the campaign.

    a. They are to disciple their "brother and sister" (new believer). Explain that Big Brothers and Big Sisters are responsible to see that the fruit is conserved.

    b. They are to make a personal visit to the persons for whom they have been praying, whether or not they have been converted.

    c. They are to begin a discipleship course with the new believer, helping him or her to become established in the Christian faith.

    d. They are to teach new believers the basics of the Christian life, such as tithing and faithfulness to church services.

    e. They are to show new believers the need for the infilling of the Holy Spirit and how to share their faith. They should explain about the power that comes through the infilling of the Holy Spirit, and so on.

    f. They are to invite new believers to the local church. (This is a key factor, as well as a biblical commandment.)

    g. They are to guide new believers toward baptism. (When they are baptized, mark it in the column of the Big Brothers and Big Sisters form.)

    h. They are to invite new believers to a membership class in the local church—doing everything possible to secure their attendance in the classes.

    i. Instruct new believers in becoming Big Brothers and Big Sisters.

CHARACTERISTICS OF BIG BROTHERS AND BIG SISTERS

1. They Pray

Prayer is the foundation of the Big Brothers and Big Sisters plan. If someone does not have the desire to pray for others, that person cannot be a Big Brother or Big Sister. The basis of this plan is not the ability to win others through persuasion, studies, or intellect. It is to win others through the love of Christ. Big Brothers and Big Sisters love people. "This is my command: love each other" (John 15:17). As a result of this love, they begin to pray for their neighbors, friends, acquaintances, and family members. They desire the best for them—that they become members of their family, the family of God.

Other things should not be neglected, such as learning a plan of salvation, building relationships with unbelievers, and gaining personal confidence. However, the most important thing is to pray for the person with whom the gospel is to be shared.

2. They Are Members of the Local Church

Big Brothers and Big Sisters are members of the local church who desire to share their faith and to win others to Christ. There are those in every congregation who are not yet involved in any ministry but are interested in learning how they can minister. These persons can participate in the Big Brothers and Big Sisters plan because it requires no previous training and gives them an opportunity to begin serving. All that is required is their willingness to learn. Jesus' disciples not only receive salvation as a gift from God but also learn how to share it. The Big Brothers and Big Sisters plan provides a system for sharing salvation.

3. They Have Taken a Basic Course in Discipleship

Big Brothers and Big Sisters prepare themselves by taking a course in discipling others. The pastor will introduce them to the available materials for discipleship (e.g., *Basic Bible Studies* by Chic Shaver [see p. 42]).

4. They Are Faithful

Big Brothers and Big Sisters are faithful to the Lord and to the church. They are interested in obeying the Lord and in growing spiritually. The author of Hebrews warns, "We must pay more careful attention, therefore, to what we have heard, so that we do not drift away" (2:1). They learn to be better disciples of Christ, remain close to Him, and seek to be filled with His Spirit.

5. They Are Willing

Big Brothers and Big Sisters are willing to go—to reach the lost and to disciple believers. God provides the power necessary to carry out this task through the fullness of the Holy Spirit in their life. Although they may be afraid like Ananias, they are still willing to say, "Here I am, Lord," and to go where He sends them.

The characteristics are illustrated in the following example. Throughout its length, the Jordan River has three notable characteristics: it receives water, it retains water, and it gives water. Because it has both an inlet and an outlet, the water contains oxygen, which supports fish and other life.

When fish enter the Dead Sea, they die for lack of oxygen and float to the surface, where they are carried away by birds. This happens because the Dead Sea, in contrast to the Jordan River, has only two of the first characteristics: It receives water and retains it, but it does not give water and has no life. For that reason, it is called the Dead Sea. Many believers *receive* the gospel but do not *give it away.* A true disciple of the Lord receives *and* gives.

Each new believer and each person for whom prayer is offered is a priceless treasure. Jesus wants their names to be written in the Book of Life. He is "not wanting anyone to perish, but everyone to come to repentance" (2 Pet. 3:9). He "wants all men to be saved and to come to the knowledge of the truth" (1 Tim. 2:4). Big Brothers and Big Sisters share Christ's burden in seeking the *lost* and discipling the *found.*

⑥ PRAYER CELLS

Aggressive church multiplication usually starts small—in small groups. From the apostles' first orientation, to their farewell meeting before His ascension, big things happened when their small group got together with Jesus. And big things still happen when Christ's disciples get together with Him! "Where two or three come together in my name, there am I with them" (Matt. 18:20).

Soul-winning plans, like Each One Win One, play an important part in releasing the spiritual skills of believers to impact communities for Christ in a first wave effort. But what's next? We sing "Onward, Christian Soldiers," but how does the army of Christ keep going? One effective way is to regroup for prayer. Prayer is the Church's greatest weapon. The spiritual power of supplication and intercession strengthens Christ's followers and enlarges their influence, which is what the early believers quickly discovered: "With great power the apostles continued to testify to the resurrection of the Lord Jesus, and much grace was upon them all" (Acts 4:33).

The church's goal shouldn't be maintenance but maximum growth, developing healthy churches that will duplicate themselves in vibrant church plants and, in turn, impact neighborhoods, regions, and entire countries. Prayer cells have been used by God throughout time to do just that. For example, prayer cells will not only build the mother church that launches them but also let her reach out and start new congregations—building the Kingdom church by church.

Church growth studies in the Church of the Nazarene show that "the increase in number of churches was a significant factor in the denomination's growth."[1] Paul Orjala shared at a missions conference that the Church "owes its record of rapid growth more to rapid church planting than to any other factor. . . . As we plant more churches, the result will be a dramatic increase in our overall growth rate." In fact, the only way we will impact the world, and fulfill the Great Commission, is by planting new churches.

So through a simple system of prayer cells people can be won to Christ, new leaders can be trained and called to preach, and new churches can be started. The prayer cell plan is designed to enable and encourage natural church growth. The successful result has been seen countless times in new, self-supporting churches. The Church of the Nazarene is using this method to multiply churches throughout the world.

THE PURPOSE OF PRAYER CELLS

The purpose of prayer cells is, first of all, to pray. There is power in prayer—personal prayer and corporate prayer. The group dynamic of a prayer cell brings people together in spirit and purpose and sends them out with hearts afire. When two of the apostles were released from the persecutor's prison, they went immediately to a prayer cell:

On their release, Peter and John went back to their own people and reported all that the chief priests and elders had said to them. When they heard this, they raised their voices together in prayer. . . . "Now, Lord, consider their threats and enable your servants

to speak your word with great boldness. Stretch out your hand to heal and perform miraculous signs and wonders through the name of your holy servant Jesus." . . . After they prayed, the place where they were meeting was shaken. And they were all filled with the Holy Spirit and spoke the word of God boldly *(Acts 4:23-24, 29-31).*
And the rest is history.

At an appointed time, for an agreed period of time, people meet together to pray for others—especially for the needs of the unchurched. Does it work? It has been discovered that about 90 percent of the prayer requests are answered by the end of each cycle of prayer cells!

Second, the purpose of prayer cells is to increase the Kingdom. As people begin to see answers to prayer in their lives, they become more open to the gospel and to the church. Established churches (mother churches) start prayer cells to reach beyond their four walls to the community—and grow in the process themselves! They grow in leadership, creating a greater support system. They grow in fellowship, inviting new people into their congregations. And they grow numerically, seeing new believers won into the Kingdom. Also, the prayer cells develop naturally into organized churches, giving the mother church a chance to decentralize and to multiply its ministry.

THE BIBLICAL BASIS FOR PRAYER CELLS

Once again, the Early Church modeled the best methods for aggressive church multiplication. Where did it start? Where did the organized church begin to take its earthly form? It took its earthy form in homes and in small groups: "They broke bread in their homes and ate together with glad and sincere hearts" (Acts 2:46). Their house meetings blossomed into organized churches.

The impact was phenomenal! God promises to reveal His plans to those who pray: "Call to me and I will answer you and tell you great and unsearchable things you do not know" (Jer. 33:3). The result of that spiritual dependence is seen in the life of the Early Church. Acts 16:5 says, "The churches were strengthened in the faith and grew daily in numbers."

This was made possible through small groups that evolved into new congregations, in the power of the Spirit. We believe that this not only can happen again but is happening right now! In South America, the power of the movement that is taking place comes exclusively from prayer. Their planning begins, continues, and ends with prayer. One pastor from the area commented that it was the first time he had seen evangelism and prayer combined in such an intricate way.

STRATEGIES FOR STARTING PRAYER CELLS

Before a pastor begins any prayer cell strategies, he or she should ask several questions: (1) How many cells should be started? (2) In what types of homes should the cells be started? (3) Where should the cell be started?

1. How Many?

It is best to begin with three or four prayer cells. First, if a church begins with only one cell, and that cell doesn't succeed, it may look as if the whole plan is doomed to failure. Second, it is easier to build enthusiasm with a larger number of cells. (However, it is usually not wise to begin with more than four, because it is more difficult to establish and evaluate that many cells.)

The goal should be to reach a point where there is a prayer cell for every 10 members. As the plan progresses, and there are more trained leaders, it is possible to manage a larger number of cells. In São Paulo, for instance, when the district had 400 members, 40 prayer cells were established. When the membership reached 600, there were 60 prayer cells. When there were 1,000 members, there were 100 prayer cells functioning.

2. In What Types of Homes?

It's advisable to begin the first prayer cells in the homes of believers. Since you are preparing an initial leadership team, it is important to look for homes where an assortment of religious doctrines is not prevalent.

Soon the cells will multiply, and then you can include homes with only one or two believers in the family. In some cases, a prayer cell may even be held in a home without any believers at all.

In one city, where the church launched a major evangelistic thrust, there were 300 members in 50 homes. Prayer cells were begun in the homes of 17 believers. Three years later, there were prayer cells in 150 homes, with 90 of those homes opening for prayer cells because *unconverted* family members had become Christians.

However, as recommended, the first leaders were trained in the homes of believers. Once they had training and experience, cells were established where only some of the members were believers. And in some cases unbelievers opened their homes because they were curious about the Christian faith. Opening cells in the homes of unbelievers usually happened only after prayer cell leaders had six to nine months of training and experience and were spiritually strong.

Targeted prayer cell sites may be classified by colors in a file, or on a map, showing
- Those where *all* persons in the home are believers
- Those where *some* persons in the home are believers
- Those where there is only *one* believer in the home
- Those where there are *sympathizers, visitors, or friends* of the church

3. Where to Meet?

It's best to locate the cells in a place where a new church could be planted. It should be a place large enough for several families, and in a home where the host family is willing to make a long-term commitment to a prayer cell—and possibly to a mission or baby church. Consideration should also be given to the distance from the mother church, the location of other cells, and the proximity to the congregation's members. It helps to pinpoint the targeted area on a map, calculating the distance between the homes and the church. (Note the distance on the map in blocks or miles.)

Since one of the purposes of prayer cells is to promote the growth of the mother church, prayer cells may be anywhere from 50 yards to 10 miles from it. Distance is not a problem. There are persons who will not attend a church even if they live on the same block with it. However, they may make contact with the church through a prayer cell.

If there are enough believers in the area, two or three cells may exist a short distance apart without a problem. This will even increase the possibility of opening a mission, especially when celebration services (see p. 65) are held in three cells. Though not all prayer cells become missions, experience tells us that out of every 10 cells, 3 become missions and that out of every 10 missions, 3 become organized churches.

WHAT HAPPENS IN THE PRAYER CELLS?

Prayer cells have several important things in common. The personalities of the cell group members may vary along with the styles and characteristics of the homes, but the prayer cells follow a common organizational pattern.

The Agenda

A prayer cell is a weekly meeting that lasts between 45 minutes to an hour. While a prayer cell agenda is not complicated, attention should be given to the proper functioning of the cell. It consists of three activities: (1) testimonies and songs of praise, (2) a chapter reading from the Book of Acts, and (3) a prayer time. Prayer is the key that makes the cell evangelistic. Each person prays—especially focusing on the spiritual needs of the unconverted. (If we only pray for believers, we have merely substituted a house, a little salt shaker, for a church building, a bigger salt shaker.) The purpose for meeting in homes is twofold: to give believers closer proximity to the unconverted and to decentralize the local church.

At a later time, prayer cell members can communicate to the unconverted that they are praying for them. This will provide a natural opportunity to invite them to the prayer cell meeting house to hear the gospel presented.

The Leaders

Prayer cells without leadership can turn into *gossip sessions with refreshments.* Trained leadership is essential to the purpose, planning, and program of the prayer cell strategy, but the plan is designed to include those who lack previous leadership experience.

There are three key leaders in every cell. They take turns leading the group, reading the Bible chapter, and writing the prayer requests in a notebook. As they rotate responsibilities each week, they will gain valuable leadership experience.

Each leader can then train two other prayer cell leaders. This will allow each cell to multiply into three cells at the end of each cycle.

The prayer cell leaders' responsibilities are as follows:

The first leader is responsible for directing the meeting. He or she will bring the group to order and lead a time of testimony and singing.

The second leader will read one chapter from the Book of Acts. (This section of the Bible is filled with church growth and Christian fellowship principles, and it also reminds cell groups of how early Christians met in house churches.)

The third leader leads the cell in prayer and keeps the prayer cell notebook. He or she records the following information:

1. Prayer requests (including those for personal needs, family members, acquaintances, and—always—the unconverted).
2. A corresponding number for each prayer request. (It is important to know how many requests there are so the number of answered prayers can be calculated later.)
3. The date of each prayer request.
4. Names, addresses, and other observations about the unconverted for whom prayers are being offered (necessary information so these persons can be invited to the evangelistic campaign).
5. Dates of answered prayers (underline the corresponding recorded prayer requests). The person who made the request should provide this information when the answer is received.
6. The chapter from the Book of Acts read in the cell group meeting that week.

WHAT TO AVOID

The success of the cell group hinges on proven principles derived from the experiences of those who have been involved in its strategy. Here are some suggestions for effective prayer cell groups:

The Cells Should Not Include Preaching or In-Depth Bible Study

Preaching or in-depth Bible study would limit the number of prayer cells. Many local churches do not have those who are qualified to preach, other than the pastor. If they were to depend on preachers to lead prayer cells, they would restrict the number of cells to the number of available preachers.

Also, these activities would limit the participation of believers who desire to be a part of the prayer cell ministry but are not gifted in preaching or teaching.

Leadership Should Not Come from Any Church but the Mother Church

Leaders from other churches could create issues about biblical doctrines and, later on, cause complications when the time comes to form a mission or new church.

Also, unconverted persons should not be prayer cell leaders. They wouldn't be familiar with the purpose of the cell.

Food or Refreshments Should Not Be Served

The preparation of refreshments puts an extra responsibility on the hosts and limits the multiplication of prayer cells because of the expected work. The objective is to pray, not eat.

The Meeting Should Not Last Longer than 45 Minutes to an Hour

Most prayer cell members work during the day, and if the meeting is too long, they likely will not attend the following week. The leaders should develop the skill of drawing the prayer cell to a close. Perhaps using a familiar line, such as, "This has been a great time of fellowship and prayer. I know we'll be looking forward to next week's meeting."

The Three Leaders Should Not Belong to Any Other Prayer Cell

Burnout is not only a hazard for vocational ministers but common among the laity as well. To avoid overload, the leaders' participation should be limited to one prayer cell. In addition, leadership issues may arise if the leaders of one cell start attending another.

Prayer Requests Should Not Be Focused on Believers' Needs Alone

Those who have been Christians for several years tend to be acquainted with more believers than unbelievers. The members of the cells must make an effort to reach out and to discover the needs of their unchurched friends. The prayer cell should avoid being member-centered. Certainly the church is to follow the advice of the apostle Paul: "Carry each other's burdens, and in this way you will fulfill the law of Christ" (Gal. 6:2). The fellowship that is expressed in times of prayer is one that strengthens the believer. But the primary purpose of the prayer cell is to focus on expanding the Kingdom, not maintaining it.

The Unconverted Should Not Be Invited

There will be a time and place when the unconverted will receive a very important invitation—to be a part of an evangelistic campaign. The prayer cell is a place where the foundation for that campaign is laid. The Bible says, "The man without the Spirit does not accept the things that come from the Spirit of God, for they are foolishness to him, and he cannot understand them, because they are spiritually discerned" (1 Cor. 2:14). Unconverted persons may not only feel uncomfortable in the prayer cell atmosphere but also not understand its purpose. At the end of the three-month cycle, they will be invited to participate in a setting where the simple claims of the gospel will be presented.

WHO IS TARGETED?

The Pastor Must Encourage Every Believer in the Mother Church to Join a Prayer Cell

The cells should be promoted constantly—from the pulpit, in the church's publications, and individually. Enthusiasm is the foundation for participation in any event, and prayer cells are no exception.

The Pastor Should Watch for Members of the Congregation Who Are Gifted in Prayer Cell Leadership

Watch for those who have demonstrated Christ in their world, are members of the local church, have leadership traits, and have an obvious desire to work.

Caution Should Be Used in Selecting Core Leadership

Among that "80 percent" of the members in most congregations who need to be involved in a ministry, such as the prayer cell, there are three basic personality types: (1) the positive, (2) the negative, and (3) the indifferent. Prayer cells need positive leadership. This next caution is also important: The established leadership of the church may have all of the qualifications—including a positive outlook—but they may have other issues. They may be bound by tradition, for instance. In that case, another search should be started. Qualified and positive leaders may be sought from newer members of the church.

Prayer Cell Leaders Should Come from the Covenant Membership of the Church

They may not be experienced, and they may not be trained in leadership principles, but potential prayer cell group leaders should be chosen from those who have proven their loyalty to Christ and to His kingdom by being committed members of a local church.

57

The Pastor Is Primary in Developing Leadership for the Prayer Cells

He or she chooses the leaders, trains them, and assigns them to their respective cells. The pastor must not delegate this action to another, because these new leaders are the pastor's disciples, so to speak. He or she personally invited them, as the Lord Jesus invited His own disciples, to accomplish a task that will result in the building of the Kingdom.

HOW IS LEADERSHIP EXPANDED?

Just as the watchmaker learns a trade by working with watches, and the carpenter by working with wood, the prayer cell leader learns by leading a cell. The leader begins to learn how to work with people, learns how to be responsible for a prayer cell, and learns to discover and use spiritual gifts. In fact, the leader can begin a lifelong ministry, preparing for other ministries while leading the cell.

The Role of the Pastor

All through this process, the pastor must stay in close contact with the leaders in training. If problems or disagreements arise, the pastor must be alert to observe every detail and to analyze the true nature of the disagreement. He or she should try to solve problems quickly so that discouragement among other leaders is avoided.

Group dynamics are very important to maintaining enthusiasm among the prayer cell leadership. The pastor will do everything possible to *encourage* the leaders. Pastors must also discipline the leaders, insisting on *commitment,* otherwise discouragement and negative attitudes will follow.

Discovering the Commitment of Leaders

The pastor will undoubtedly have to deal with some prayer cell leaders who are not committed. This is a time of training and testing. The pastor should be on the alert for signs that a prayer cell leader is not fulfilling his or her responsibilities. Tardiness, lack of organization, or a lack of preparation are key indicators. In a spirit of Christian love, the pastor should discuss the leader's responsibilities with the leader, reminding him or her of the covenant that was made in the beginning. The leader should also be reminded that his or her first allegiance is to Christ—and to the building of Christ's kingdom.

It is advisable that the host of the home where a cell group meets not be the leader of that cell. It would be more advisable for a leader to preside over a cell in another home—even a home in another area. It is actually better when a leader lives in another neighborhood. It may be more inconvenient, but it develops discipline that helps to prepare the leader.

Multiplying Leaders

Where there are three leaders, and each performs a different task, they are training each other. After the first cycle, the three leaders may be separated. One may stay in the same house and help train two new leaders. The other two may go to different homes and help train two more leaders in each home. In this way, not only cells but also leaders are multiplied.

At the end of the second cycle, there will be three cells led by the original three leaders, plus six new leaders. The multiplication continues so that after each cycle, each leader takes the responsibility of discipling two new leaders, teaching them what he or she has learned.

Finally, when the pastor divides the leaders among the cells, he or she should try to have one man and two women or vice versa. If a husband and wife are leaders, they should always be in the same cell.

THE DISCIPLESHIP CELL (THE MOTHER CELL)

The foundation of the prayer cell system is the *discipleship cell.* This cell is comprised of all prayer cell leaders, along with the pastor. Its purpose is to give inspiration, guidance, and motivation to the leaders.

This may be the most important meeting in the pastor's week. It is the time when the pastor disciples the leaders. There are five elements in the discipleship process, and each of these should be included in the meetings.

1. The Leaders Should Be Given Solid Spiritual Food Through Bible Study

This will not only help them develop spiritual depth but will also give them an understanding of the church's biblical mission.

2. Prayer Cell Strategies Should Be Taught

The leaders need to understand the purpose and procedures of prayer cells, the rotation of responsibilities, the use of the notebook, and ways that the cells can influence the establishing of a mission, or even the planting of a new church.

3. The Leaders Should Be Motivated to Carry Out the Church's Mission

They must understand the importance of what they are doing in the context of the overall mission of the mother church. Encouragement and praise, as well as direction, should come from the pastor in a spirit of enthusiasm and excitement. Leaders are revived and encouraged in the mother cell. In return, their revival and encouragement is caught by the rest of prayer cells.

4. Leaders Need to Ask Questions and Discuss Problems

The mother cell is an opportunity for the leader to learn from the experience and wisdom of the mother cell leader—the pastor. It also gives them an opportunity to learn from the experiences of other leaders. Each problem is different, but all problems share the same causes and cures.

5. There Should Be an Evaluation of What Is Taking Place in Each of the Prayer Cells

Leaders should give an account of the progress (or lack of it) in their cells. Suggestions may be made that will help steer the cells in the right direction. And suggestions may also be made that will help the leaders improve their leadership skills.

Also, the evaluation time can be a time of encouragement. For instance, the prayer cell leaders should bring their prayer request notebooks to this meeting. The reading of answered prayer requests can be a great source of encouragement to the other leaders and propel them on to even greater commitments to the purpose of the prayer cell strategy.

The discipleship cells (mother cells) can be structured so that the leaders will receive the broadest training possible. Below is an example of possible themes for six months of discipleship cells. Robert Wade, who pastor's in Grand Junction, Colorado, used these:

1. Power of God to answer prayer
2. Purpose and plan of prayer cells
3. Importance of the evangelism team
4. Christ's concern for the unsaved
5. Plan of accountability
6. A Bible study on the "Heart of a Leader"
7. Personal evangelism
8. Basic doctrine
9. Making God's Word yours
10. Pointing to the crusade
11. Altar work
12. Follow-up
13. How to pray for the unsaved

14. Maintaining personal spiritual focus
15. Spirit-filled life
16. Sanctify yourself/take up your cross
17. Power of faith
18. Developing faith
19. Praying in faith
20. Praying for healing
21. Praying for physical security, jobs, and finances
22. Praying for families
23. Praying for cell leaders

While the main purpose of the discipleship cell is discipling new leaders, there are other benefits as well. It builds a *team* that supports the successes (or setbacks) of each member. It also provides a sense of accountability. It is, in fact, crucial to the success of the system.

BENEFITS OF A PRAYER CELL

The list of the benefits a local church may derive from the prayer cell strategy is great. Among the most important:

1. It stimulates the development of workers. They begin to discover their gifts and ministries.
2. The church and the pastor are decentralized.
3. Prayer is systematically offered for specific needs. James says, "When you ask, you do not receive, because you ask with wrong motives" (James 4:3).
4. There is growth in the local church. Participants of the cells will usually attend the mother church on Sunday.

The next chapter will explain how the prayer cells can be used to prepare for evangelistic campaigns. Since it is recommended that local churches have an evangelistic campaign every six months, some pastors have found that it is natural to repeat the cycle of prayer cells on that same schedule.

IV.

HARVEST

⑦ EVANGELISTIC CAMPAIGNS

Perhaps you've heard it said, "Evangelistic campaigns just don't work anymore." Sadly, that false assessment has been widely accepted. A true assessment might be, Perhaps in some places evangelistic campaigns don't work. But if the research were done, in many of those places campaigns don't work because the church isn't willing to *do the work in advance.*

Evangelistic campaigns aren't like self-cleaning ovens. You don't just throw stuff in the calendar and expect everything to turn out right. You don't just unlock the church or auditorium doors, flip on the light switch, and expect the place to be filled. Evangelistic campaigns take perspiration as well as inspiration. Colossians 3:23-24 says, "Whatever you do, work at it with all your heart, as working for the Lord, not for men, since you know that you will receive an inheritance from the Lord as a reward. It is the Lord Christ you are serving."

Of course we can't order a revival. God isn't at our disposal. He is a sovereign God, and true revival is poured out on the church in His sovereign timing. But He is also a merciful God who wants people to be saved *right now.* As 2 Pet. 3:9 says, "The Lord is not slow in keeping his promise, as some understand slowness. He is patient with you, not wanting anyone to perish, but everyone to come to repentance." What is the promise that goes along with the plea? "Come near to God and he will come near to you. Wash your hands, you sinners, and purify your hearts, you double-minded" (James 4:8).

The principles are here. First, He doesn't want anyone to perish. Second, He wants men, women, boys, girls—everyone—to come into the safety of His kingdom. Third, if we'll meet His conditions, He'll act in accordance to His will. He'll stop by our churches, our auditoriums, our tents, our homes, and best of all, our hearts. He'll pour out His Spirit on the hurting and the hungering. He'll draw people to himself—even through the programs of His people.

He wants not only the unconverted to be saved but also the believers to be sanctified—to be separated from the world—filled and empowered by His Holy Spirit. "But just as he who called you is holy, so be holy in all you do; for it is written: 'Be holy, because I am holy'" (1 Pet. 1:15-16). God doesn't smile on empty altars and half-filled churches any more than He smiles on empty spirits and half-filled hearts. He wants to send showers of blessing. He wants to see a harvest—now!

Evangelists shouldn't be preaching to the faithful few who are dedicated enough to show up for spring and fall scheduled meetings. If the church will *plan the evangelistic campaign,* and *campaign for the plan,* there can be an abundant harvest. It's still happening. Auditoriums and stadiums are still being filled with people hungry for the gospel. As a result, churches are building multi-thousand-seat auditoriums. Why? Because there is an ever-increasing hunger for God. What was supposed to have worked in peoples' lives—careers, possessions, fame, accomplishments—hasn't worked. There is a place marked "reserved for God" in the hearts of people everywhere.

Harvest now! It's the church's finest opportunity. It's time to pull out the spiritual stops. It's time for an evangelistic campaign—in your church, in your neighborhood, in your community, in your region, or in your country. And you can be the leader of the pack!

The church in South America was confronted with the familiar problem of holding meetings for the faithful few. But instead of accepting it, they set out to find an answer for it. They launched evangelistic campaigns. What was the result? Unsaved people attended, and now they frequently have over 100 converts in a very short campaign.[1]

There are additional results. Believers are revived and involved in discipling new converts and leading prayer cells. There is a renewed desire to see the unconverted won to Christ. Leaders are being called into vocational service. Missions are being started. New churches are being planted. Lives are being transformed.

And it all started with an evangelistic campaign.

HOW EVANGELISTIC CAMPAIGNS WORK

Evangelistic campaigns work best when they are the focal point of an in-depth time of preparation. In the two previous plans that we have presented, Big Brothers and Big Sisters and prayer cells, much of the harvest takes place during evangelistic campaigns. Those evangelistic strategies are designed to bring the unsaved to hear the gospel. Notice how they dovetail with a scheduled campaign.

Big Brothers and Big Sisters

Two months prior to the church's spring and fall campaigns, participants in the Big Brothers and Big Sisters plan are consecrated. They begin praying for 10 unsaved people whom they plan to invite to the campaign. During that time, they also are being trained to teach a basic course in discipleship, which will be taught to those who will accept Christ.

Implementing the plan, 1 out of every 10 who are being prayed for will usually attend the evangelistic campaign. Approximately one-third of those unsaved people who attend will accept Christ. During the preparation for a two-day campaign in one region, 500 people were praying for 5,000 friends. The result was 500 unsaved friends attending and 162 accepting Christ!

The reason it works so well is that it gives participants two months to prepare to ask the unconverted to attend the campaign. As Big Brothers and Big Sisters pray each day—for 60 days—for the people on their list, their desire to see these unsaved loved ones, friends, and associates won to the Lord will naturally increase. Or putting it another way, after they have knocked on the door of heaven that many times, they are ready to knock on the doors of the unconverted and invite them to hear the gospel!

Through their daily prayer, the Holy Spirit has already been working in the hearts of those on their top 10 list. Many Big Brothers and Big Sisters have shared how God has given them unusual opportunities to invite others.

Many of your own people could be enlisted to bring the unconverted to an evangelistic campaign, and you can be assured that a high percentage of those who are invited will be open to receiving Christ.

Prayer Cells

Prayer cells are also used to bring new people to the campaign. In fact, the evangelistic campaign begins on the prayer cell level. At least three months before the campaign, cells are organized. They begin to pray for the campaign and also for the needs of unsaved friends. Three weeks prior to the campaign, those unsaved persons who were being prayed for in the cell are invited to a celebration at the house where the prayer cell is being held.

In this meeting, the prayer notebook is displayed, showing the names of the people and the various requests for which the cell group members have been praying. Most will be underlined in red, indicating that the prayer requests have been answered. This will have two positive effects on the guests: (1) it will show them that Christians are genuinely interested in their needs; (2) it will show them that God answers prayer.

There will be prayers and songs of praise for what God has done. The celebration service may end with a gospel presentation, giving guests the opportunity to receive Christ. It is natural to invite those who attend this meeting to attend the campaign, which is set to begin in a few days. And those who accepted Christ will be encouraged to bring someone to the campaign.

The prayer cells and the Big Brothers and Big Sisters plans make it possible for the church to capitalize on what research has shown as "the most effective means of capturing the interest of the unchurched . . . a personal invitation from a friend."[2] The emphasis is where it should be, not on a program and not on the charisma of a speaker, but on depending on God in prayer.

The evangelistic campaign makes a great impact because the work has been done. Nothing has been taken for granted. The campaign plan has been planned, and the plans have been campaigned. And more, the hearts of believers have been opened to God's call; consecrated believers have made a commitment to reaching the lost; discipled *disciplers* have been trained to teach new converts; entire groups of people have been praying—and believing—that God would transform the lives of people on their prayer list; and the unconverted have been invited to attend.

The results will not be unlike those of an Early Church evangelistic campaign, where the apostle Peter was the evangelist:

> Peter [preached], "Repent and be baptized, every one of you, in the name of Jesus Christ for the forgiveness of your sins. And you will receive the gift of the Holy Spirit. The promise is for you and your children and for all who are far off—for all whom the Lord our God will call." With many other words he warned them; and he pleaded with them, "Save yourselves from this corrupt generation." Those who accepted his message were baptized, and about three thousand were added to their number that day *(Acts 2:38-41)*.

PLANNING FOR AN EVER-INCREASING HARVEST

Successful evangelistic campaigns need months of preparation. And the results of those campaigns—the harvest—need careful *conservation*. The process can become a cycle of sowing and reaping in which the church is continually involved, until it becomes a regular part of the church's outreach ministry. Below is a calendar of *preparation* and *conservation* that may be included in the process of reaping an ever-increasing harvest: a countdown to the campaign.

Six Months in Advance

Assuming that the church has just finished an evangelistic campaign and will be conducting another in six months, the church again implements the Big Brothers and Big Sisters and prayer cell plans. Their responsibilities include the following:

1. Big Brothers and Big Sisters should begin working with those who have accepted Christ, leading them through the *Basic Bible Studies* (see p. 42). Also, they should introduce new believers

to others in the local church and encourage them to develop regular attendance at the church's services.

2. The pastor should invite new converts to baptism classes, where the meaning of baptism and church membership will be explained. As soon as possible, a service of baptism should be scheduled. A service to receive members into the church should also be scheduled for the following month.

3. The pastor should preach a Sunday night sermon series on the same themes that the Big Brothers and Big Sisters are teaching new converts in their *Basic Bible Studies.* (These should be simple, practical sermons that will reinforce what new converts need to know to begin their Christian life.)

4. An afternoon fellowship meal should be scheduled for the Sunday following the campaign. This should be a time for new converts and church members to get acquainted. (A special effort should be made to introduce the new converts to as many members of the church as possible.) The informal atmosphere of the fellowship meal is a great opportunity for the new converts to see that Christians are real people, that they have real challenges and victories, and that they are one big family.

The fellowship meal is also an opportunity to minister to the extended family of the new converts. Activities should be planned for children, illustrating the church's concern for the young members of the new convert's family.

5. The pastor should begin follow-up meetings with the Big Brothers and Big Sisters. These meetings are designed to discuss the progress of the new converts (and to pray for them) and to give further training in discipleship.

6. Prayer cells that have been operating for the past three months should be evaluated to see which may become missions and which have the possibilities for becoming new churches. Details are given in this book for developing *cells* into *missions,* and missions into *new churches* (see chapter 8).

7. A new cycle of prayer cells should be launched. (See chapter 6.)
- A local coordinator should be appointed.
- Areas of the community should be targeted.
- Homes/meeting places should be chosen.
- Leaders should be trained and assigned.

Five Months in Advance

1. The pastor should receive into the church as members new converts who have completed the membership class.

2. The church should reimplement the Each One Win One plan, with the pastor preaching in advance a series of messages on the church's responsibility for the harvest. Opportunities should be given for additional members of the church to become involved in the soul-winning and discipleship process.

3. Big Brothers and Big Sisters should continue to work with the new Christians in the *Basic Bible Studies.* The pastor should give public recognition to those who have completed the studies.

4. The pastor should continue to promote prayer cells and to lead the discipleship cell.

5. The pastor should regularly remind the congregation of the need to win the lost and to use the Each One Win One poster.

Four Months in Advance

1. New members should be guided in discovering and using their spiritual gifts in ministry. Spiritual-gift tests may be given. Midweek and/or Sunday evening services would be ideal times to teach new believers (and established believers) about the responsibility for building the Kingdom by using their spiritual gifts.

2. The pastor should promote the Theological Education by Extension program, especially with those in the discipleship cell and those who are leading missions.

3. The pastor should preach on the infilling of the Holy Spirit, encouraging Christians to seek this experience.

4. Big Brothers and Big Sisters should continue to do their work—to disciple new Christians by modeling the life of a growing Christian; by continuing to spend time with them; and by doing all they can to encourage, motivate, and teach them.

5. Prayer cells should be evaluated, monitoring the number of prayer requests for the unconverted. Leaders should be encouraged and motivated. And public recognition should be given to those who are participating in the plan.

Three Months in Advance

1. The pastor and leaders should be on the alert for those who are not attending the church services regularly. They should be visiting them and finding out how the church can meet their needs.

2. A date should be set for the consecration of Big Brothers and Big Sisters at the beginning of next month.

3. The church should design and print posters, flyers, and Big Brothers and Big Sisters forms for the campaign.

4. The pastor should preach on the need to impact the city for Christ.

5. There should be an evaluation of the prayer cells, noting which have been praying for enough unsaved people to have a celebration service. There should also be an evaluation of which cells could become missions and which missions could become new churches.

Two Months in Advance

1. New Big Brothers and Big Sisters should be consecrated. (See chapter 5.)

2. The church should continue to display the Each One Win One poster.

3. The pastor/coordinator should train Big Brothers and Big Sisters in discipling new converts.

4. To involve as many people as possible, coordinators should be appointed to organize workers for advertising, programming, and transportation for the evangelistic campaign.

5. The pastor should promote the Big Brothers and Big Sisters plan weekly, encouraging Big Brothers and Big Sisters to pray daily and encouraging others to become a part of the plan.

6. The evangelistic campaign should be promoted.

7. Prayer cell celebration services should be scheduled and preachers selected who will present the gospel in each of the celebration services.

One Month in Advance

1. Altar workers should be trained in the use of the decision cards used in registering those who make a decision.

2. The church should canvass the surrounding neighborhoods with the information about the evangelistic campaign—distributing attractive and colorful flyers or brochures that will describe the basic information about it.

3. Celebration services should be conducted in the prayer cells, assigning workers to disciple those who accepted Christ and inviting people to the campaign service(s).

4. Big Brothers and Big Sisters should be asked to invite each of the top 10 for whom they have been praying.

5. The multiplication of prayer cells should be planned, determining where they will be and who will be the leaders.

Conduct the Evangelistic Campaign

Plan the services to be enthusiastic, practical, and heartwarming. Prepare the speaker to give an invitation. Have immediate follow-up material on hand. And expect results!

RESULTS OF AN EVANGELISTIC CAMPAIGN

In a church that repeats this cycle twice a year, a pattern of members involved in winning others will develop. The Each One Win One model will soon become more than a slogan to the church.

Since we began these plans of preparing for evangelistic campaigns and discipling the new converts, church membership in the South American churches has increased by over 200 percent. Your church can also experience this accelerated increase of members, as you continue to impact your area for Christ.

Not only is there an increase in members, but there is also an increase in leaders. Through the prayer cells and the pastor's discipleship cell, laypersons will be trained. And many will go on to become leaders in other ministry areas, including missions and new churches.

Accelerated church multiplication will result. Many of the prayer cells will enjoy celebration services, where people are saved. Prayer cells will choose to continue meeting as a mission. And missions will become churches.

CITYWIDE EVANGELISTIC CAMPAIGN

As churches begin to plant other churches, and the vision to impact entire neighborhoods grows, a spirit of cooperation among churches will evolve. In this spirit of spiritual enthusiasm, it is possible to take the evangelistic campaigns to the next level—a citywide campaign.

The district superintendent and the district IMPACT coordinator (this task will be discussed later in chapter 9) may organize participating churches in a city to implement Big Brothers and Big Sisters and prayer cell plans in a coordinated effort while conducting celebration services and local church campaigns. The weekend after the local church campaigns, a citywide campaign may be held.

Envision Big Brothers and Big Sisters from several churches inviting their top 10 lists; prayer cells inviting new converts; and local churches bringing their friends, families, and associates to an evangelistic service! Also, envision each local church canvassing a thousand homes. The result could be an auditorium or stadium-filled meeting!

In one three-night citywide campaign, eight small- to medium-sized churches worked together to lead over 300 people to Christ!

Yes, evangelistic campaigns still work—if they are worked. And they will continue to be one of God's great tools for using the spiritual skills of believers, evangelizing the lost, and impacting the entire world for Christ. (See Appendix H.)

⑧ MULTIPLYING CHURCHES AND PASTORS

The Early Church had a mind-set that contributed greatly to its growth. Perhaps it is best seen in Luke's account: "All the believers were together and had everything in common. Selling their possessions and goods, they gave to anyone as he had need" (Acts 2:44-45). In this age of ecclesiastical one-upmanship, that would be a rarity indeed. When was the last time you heard of a growing church foregoing a building project to give building fund money to another growing church?

The Early Church was more concerned with mission than medals. The cause of Christ was paramount. It took precedence over individual or corporate gain. Christ modeled self-sacrifice in such a magnificent way that His followers were duty bound to react if one of their fellow believers had a need. That spirit of cooperation was like a forest fire—it burned away all pretense and self-seeking. And the fire spread, resulting in accelerated church growth and accelerated church planting. People by the thousands wanted to be a part of that kind of family.

First-century Christians simply followed the example of their Savior and that of their spiritual patriarchs. John's copycat Christianity was evident in his writings: "And this is his command: to believe in the name of his Son, Jesus Christ, and to love one another as he commanded us" (1 John 3:23). It was a love that took out a loan if a brother or sister in faith needed it.

That cooperative spirit is still alive in the church, though it needs a spiritual transfusion once in a while! Churches are working together. In many places, they are combining ministries and methods to reach the lost and strengthen believers. But just imagine the next level! Imagine what the *entire church* of the living Christ could accomplish if no one cared who got the credit?

Church growth couldn't be contained!

Where there is a selfless spirit of cooperation among pastors and churches in a city, there is a tremendous possibility that the entire city—and region—could be impacted for Christ. A veritable shopping list of church growth options would unfurl:

- Citywide evangelistic campaigns
- Ongoing leadership training
- Effective compassionate ministries
- Quality broadcasting
- High-impact advertising
- Cooperative design and building projects
- Life-changing recovery programs
- Continual church planting

Churches in some overseas regions, for instance, have developed just that spirit of cooperation. In the process, they have acquired a vision that goes beyond the local church. They are planting churches throughout their communities and sending out new pastors from their congregations—and from their daughter congregations.

To this point, we have presented evangelistic strategies that can be used to build the local church. It is our hope that they will be widely used for God's glory. But there's a next level. We will have to ramp-up our church growth strategies if we are to reach our *whole world* for Christ. We will have to look beyond the local church, to aggressively impact entire cities.

In this chapter we will present ways that several churches in one city, several churches in one district, or several districts can cooperate to train and send new pastors and plant new churches.

Be forewarned. There will be a huge cost involved!

Church leaders who are threatened by the success of others or who want to hoard their best personnel or programs will have to make a major shift and a complete transformation of their former church growth thinking. In the spirit of John Wesley, the world is our parish.

Also, district organizations that regard church planting as a district responsibility will need to rethink their philosophies. In this accelerated strategy, the team's the thing! Actually, Kingdom building is not only a team sport but also a contact sport! That's not to make light of our history, our calling, or our objective. But we're at war—at war with the enemy of the church and its harvest. Church leaders—local or district—must be motivated to take a good look through their own church windows or their own district office windows to a field that is whitened to harvest.

Sometimes it will mean turning over the church growth keys. It might mean that we will have to listen and learn, instead of giving out marching orders—to be taught as well as to teach.

No, we're not calling for an abandonment of general or district church organization or authority. Churches simply cannot grow without authoritative leadership. We're calling for a *reinvention* of church growth, by giving the primary responsibility for planting new churches back to the local church. This is a call to work as a team for the advancement of the Kingdom so that the will of God will be done on earth as it is in heaven.

Let's look at some vital (and in some cases, new) solutions for empowering the local church for accelerated church multiplication.

EACH CHURCH PLANT A CHURCH

In previous chapters, we presented the first stages of the prayer cell plan. We suggested that they benefit the local church, first, as an *army of prayer warriors* who see the unconverted won to Christ and, second, as *training ground for new leaders*. They serve as a base for reaching the unchurched and launching evangelistic campaigns.

Many prayer cells will have served their purpose when they have completed the first stages. However, some cells will implement two more stages: third, they will start a mission and, fourth, they will plant a new church.

The Mission

Whether a prayer cell will enter the next stage and grow into a mission can actually be decided by those attending the cell's celebration service. At the end of the service the pastor should explain that this prayer cell is ending.

The pastor should then ask if there is interest in continuing to have services on a particular weekday evening. A vote should be taken. If it is affirmative (and it usually is), a mission is established. Since this little congregation made this important decision, they will naturally have a sense of ownership. And they will more likely be faithful in attendance. Perhaps you would like to call the new, extended meetings a fellowship rather than a mission.

The mission will then continue meeting for one hour each week, always in the same place. Mission meetings should be similar to a worship service, with music, prayer, testimonies, offerings, teaching, and preaching. The group will include new believers reached through the prayer cell, church members who were originally involved in the cell, and other friends and neighbors. Those who attend the weekday mission meetings should be encouraged to faithfully attend the Sunday services of the mother church. The mother church supervises, motivates, and encourages its new daughter.

The New Church

The transition to the fourth stage, new church, will take place as a group identity develops within the mission. The group meets regularly, forms a family bond, and plans other activities together. Small groups seem to naturally plan for additional meetings and activities, because everyone feels significant and wants to be involved. The mission will grow and may even launch its own prayer cells—cells that will not only strengthen its members but also provide new people to attend its meetings.

After a mission has met for several months, it will begin to take on the characteristics and atmosphere of a *church*. That is the time for the mission to schedule its own Sunday services. Then if there is a similar positive response to these services, the pastor of the mother church should advise and encourage the mission to become a church. Upon the agreement of the mission members, the pastor should then invite the district superintendent to organize the new church. The mother church, the pastor, and the district superintendent will continue to oversee, resource, and encourage this new daughter.

The time will come when the new church congregation will be limited by the size of the house in which it is meeting. The group should then consider renting a larger facility. As the congregation continues to grow, they will want to consider buying or building their own church building.

It is important to recognize the order in which these steps take place:

1. Prayer cells grow into a mission through trained prayer cell leadership.
2. Mission leaders are trained.
3. The mission is established.
4. The mission grows by establishing its own prayer cells.
5. New attendees are invited to become a part of the mission.
6. The mission is given the opportunity to become its own church.
7. The new church is organized and meets in rented facilities.
8. The new church continues to grow and buys or builds a church building.

Anything missing? Let's take a look!

- Lots of prayer by members of the mother church and the cell/mission/new church
- Continual supervision and resourcing by the mother church pastor
- Opportunities for fellowship with the mother church
- Encouragement for the new church to start its own outreach

This strategy of natural church planting and growth enables new churches to start without outside funding. There is really no limit to the number of churches that can be started in this way. Each church can set a goal of starting another church. And each church *can reach that goal* by implementing the stages outlined.

NEW CHURCH PASTORS

It is a glorious thing to see prayer cells develop into new churches. However, as it is with every growing organization, there are unique personnel and program challenges. New methods must be tried, new staff must be found, and there must be ongoing training.

Where do the pastors of these new churches come from? The problem of finding the right pastor for a new church is one of the challenges in this strategy for multiplying churches.

The "Growing Church" Problem

Three important questions need to be answered if qualified pastors are to staff new and growing churches:

First, where will the new church get the resources to provide for its minister? There is no parsonage, and there probably are not enough members to pay a full-time pastor. The answer is obvious—pastors of these new churches must be willing to be bivocational, at least in the beginning.

Second, how will the new pastor fit into the new church? He or she will not be coming into a typical church setting. These churches may have a strong relationship with the mother church and its pastor. They also will have a different church mentality. Many of their members will not have the spiritual upbringing or tradition of ministry that established members might have. The answer is the new pastor will have to be uniquely trained in knowing how to lead them. (See the new solution at the end of this chapter.)

A third question looms—how can we have a movement that multiplies a large number of churches when there are fewer young people entering the ministry? In most denominations, the number of ministerial students is on the decline. The answer to this question is found in our discussion of Paul's advice to Pastor Timothy: "You then, my son, be strong in the grace that is in Christ Jesus. And the things you have heard me say in the presence of many witnesses entrust to reliable men who will also be qualified to teach others" (2 Tim. 2:1-2).

Just as the Each One Win One plan multiplies believers, and the prayer cell and Big Brothers and Big Sisters plans multiply churches, pastors must multiply their ministries by developing new pastors.

The New Solution

As Paul suggested, the solution is right in our own backyards. We'll grow our own pastors!

- It is a solution to each problem we have just noted.
- It is a solution that would bring many new ministerial students to Bible colleges, regional colleges, and seminaries.
- It is a solution that would provide a pastor for every new church we open—a pastor who already has a job in the community and is willing to be bivocational.

Laypersons in our own churches are potential pastors for new churches. There are several positive reasons for this: (1) they already have a close relationship with the mother church and pastor; (2) perhaps most important, they have been involved in the new church from the beginning and understand those who are involved; and (3) they are eager to see the new church move toward becoming a healthy, growing church that will plant other churches.

This new solution is a proven solution, with its roots in the Early Church. It has a clear goal—to recruit and train pastors out of the mother church or out of the new church. The only thing that remains is to see how it's done. Here is the process:

1. As each pastor trains leaders in the discipleship cell and gives them responsibilities in church leadership, he or she will identify some of these leaders as potential pastors by their gifts and motivation.

2. The pastor can then give these potential pastors the opportunity to lead missions. As the pastor gives these mission leaders more attention and even greater opportunities to serve, two things will be revealed: first, that God is calling them to preach and, second, that they will need further theological education. (Each pastor probably has at least one leader in the congregation whom God is calling to preach.)

This process has taken place hundreds of times in areas where the strategies we have mentioned have been implemented. As new pastors come up through mother churches, there will always be enough leaders for daughter churches.

These are leaders the pastor knows well. They have been tested throughout the process. They can be placed strategically in the missions where they will best be able to minister. So, the problem of bringing in an unknown minister should not even exist. It is virtually certain that the homegrown pastor and the new congregation will have the same goals and expectations, and there will be no rude awakenings for either.

In addition, there won't be the need for more funds to move, house, insure, and pay a new minister. The pastor will already have a secular job and a home. This means he or she may already have many relationships in the community that will provide excellent harvest fields.

The solution of having each pastor train another pastor decentralizes the mother church pastor. And the ministry of that pastor is multiplied many times over when he or she invests time and energy in training new leaders.

District superintendents play an important role in recognizing these leaders as pastors. They must trust the referral from the mother church and work with its pastor to disciple and train the new pastor.

Some new pastors will fail, but the percentage will be no higher than in our present system. And those who do not succeed as pastors can move back into another ministry in the local church without being scarred by failure in the pastorate. Yes, there is a risk in such a rapid multiplication of pastors, but it is worth it. We encourage you to trust God, step out on faith, and try it!

SUPPORT SYSTEMS

Obviously, the addition of new churches and the ongoing need for new pastors will demand even greater resources. But much of the system already exists—not only in new plans for equipping laypersons to become bivocational and vocational pastors but also in systems that have already been put in place by the denomination of the mother church.

Education by Extension

We must put a high priority on education, especially on having educated ministers. We have already mentioned the need for bringing theological training *to* the pastors—by opening education centers in the areas where there are established ministries. In days past, it was thought that the only option for training pastors was for them to *go* to a Bible college or to a regional college and on to seminary. The mind-set was that only after the completion of three to seven years of theological education could a person begin pastoring.

Now clearly continuing education is a necessity and seminary training should always be encouraged, but if churches are going to impact their world with the gospel, they must use all of their options—including Education by Extension—to prepare more pastors than are currently studying in their colleges and universities.

One proven solution is on-the-job training, allowing pastors to receive their education while pastoring and maintaining a secular job. This permits leaders who have been raised up in the mother church to begin pastoring a daughter church immediately.

The plan of Education by Extension may differ from a denomination's study course in that students actually attend classes with other students and have an instructor. The classes may be held in centers throughout a district, at a time and place that allows as many students as possible to participate. The denomination, or its district (District Ministerial Studies Board), may appoint the best teachers available for each course. Also, a high academic standard can be maintained by adding lectures by video, DVD, or teleconferencing. District-appointed teachers could lead the on-site discussions and grade homework and tests.

Involving the Educational Institutions

Bible colleges, regional colleges and universities, and seminaries could help with the preparation of audiovisual presentations and with the appointment of district teachers. In fact, the educational institutions of a denomination could establish their own Education by Extension tracks. Districts will gain students from this program, enrollment in the educational institutions will increase, and the potential for more students will widen.

There is not a shortage of people who are called by God into the ministry. There is only a shortage of those who respond. The system of churches planting churches, and pastors training pastors, enables and encourages gifted laypersons to respond to the call. As lay leaders are involved in starting missions and churches, they will see the need for additional ministers—for being open personally to the call of God.

Opportunities for Educational Institutions

Some who are called will feel there is no way they can prepare for the ministry. They have their own careers and ministries. They have families and homes to care for and financial obligations. They may even be beyond college age. Education by Extension can help tear down those barriers. There wouldn't be a need to uproot individuals or families—no need to move to another city for training and a more expensive education. A person of any age, from a teenager to a senior citizen, can be involved.

But there is also an advantage for educational institutions.

When these people answer the call of God and are already pastoring, most will see the value of continuing their training beyond the Education by Extension program. The educational institutions of the denomination will receive the fruit of this program. New church pastor-students will be motivated to further their education.

Education by Extension will provide a new entry level for the ministry—and a new opportunity for educational institutions. Prayer cell and mission leaders will be motivated to go on to higher education.

Added Benefits of Education by Extension

As an added advantage, after the pastor-student has completed the Education by Extension program and entered the higher education system, his or her church may have reached a financial position to call a full-time pastor. Here is one more benefit to include with those already mentioned. Using and training a homegrown pastor can provide time—time needed for a new church to grow and flourish, time for it to stand on its own feet. That's something that's hard to beat.

There is a great need for this new level of entry into the ministry. It will require effort by the pastors of mother churches, but most will enjoy sharing their wisdom and experience with those who are entering the ministry. It is rewarding to multiply your ministry by training new pastors and multiplying churches.

⑨ IMPACT: COORDINATING THE PLANS

We have presented several plans for accelerated church multiplication: Each One Win One, Big Brothers and Big Sisters, prayer cells, and evangelistic campaigns. Each of these can not only be implemented at the local level, building the local church and starting missions and new churches, but they can also be used to "impact" a city, a region, or even an entire country!

The purpose of this chapter is to explain the coordination of the plans on a citywide level, in what we call IMPACT (Involving Members, Pastors, And Churches in Tandem).

Webster's says that "in tandem" means "acting in conjunction." When God's people are acting in tandem, that is, working together, they can make an even greater impact on their world. Paul advised the Early Church to avoid division over personal loyalties and territory by *acting in conjunction* to build the Kingdom:

> What, after all, is Apollos? And what is Paul? Only servants, through whom you came to believe—as the Lord has assigned to each his task. I planted the seed, Apollos watered it, but God made it grow. So neither he who plants nor he who waters is anything, but only God, who makes things grow. The man who plants and the man who waters have one purpose, and each will be rewarded according to his own labor. For we are God's fellow workers; you are God's field, God's building *(1 Cor. 3:5-9)*.

IMPACT LEADERSHIP

Every great evangelistic effort begins with dedicated and focused leaders who exemplify a cooperative spirit. For example, Christ's disciples first worked together; then they ventured out individually or in pairs to evangelize the lost and to establish new missions and new churches. The energy they received, first from being with Christ and then from being in the group, motivated them to new and exciting ministries around the world—in a spirit of cooperation.

The evangelism and discipleship plans we have studied can only succeed with good leadership. It's the same when coordinating the plans to make an even wider impact on a city, region, or country. From revitalizing the local church to sparking revival in other parts of the world, someone must direct the operation.

We should say at the outset that in those denominations that have a form of government that includes district leadership, those leaders play a key role in the success of IMPACT; they must be 100 percent involved. For example, the district superintendent helps in setting the goals and giving motivation to the pastors under his or her supervision.

However, IMPACT begins in the local church. The local church is the strength of the program. The focus on church multiplication that helps to launch Each One Win One, Big Brothers and Big Sisters, prayer cells, and evangelistic campaigns starts with the vision of the local congregation. Thus the cooperation and leadership of the local church pastor are also vital to the success of the citywide effort.

The core leadership of IMPACT is the coordinator. Someone must be the player-coach. Someone must be responsible for carrying out the assignments that will result in influencing a local community for Christ. Coordinators may be of different gender, age, or experience, but they will have certain characteristics in common. To be successful, the coordinators/leaders of IMPACT must have at least three essential character traits:

1. Humility

It says in 1 Pet. 5:5, "Clothe yourselves with humility toward one another, because, 'God opposes the proud but gives grace to the humble.'" Successful leadership always begins with successful follow-ship. A coordinated effort to impact an entire community will demand cooperation with an established line of authority. God moves through the line and staff of the organization. Each person recognizes the authority and responsibility of the other.

2. Faithfulness

Pastor Paul said, "Now it is required that those who have been given a trust must prove faithful" (1 Cor. 4:2). That means being faithful to the leadership of the Holy Spirit, faithful to the teachings of the Word of God, faithful to the doctrine of the parent church, and faithful to the responsibilities of leadership. Faithfulness is not optional. Jesus said, "Be faithful, even to the point of death, and I will give you the crown of life" (Rev. 2:10). God does not ask us to be successful, only to be faithful. He works through our faithfulness to accomplish His purpose.

3. Hardworking

Leaders must be committed to hard work. Kingdom building isn't a piece of cake. It's tiring, frustrating, and often humbling. The church of the living Christ is built on the sweat of its members as well as their tears. Jesus promised us that we would have triumphs, but He also said that we would have tribulation.

THE IMPACT PLAN

We suggest a four-stage schedule for starting the IMPACT plan. (And once it is started, it should continue.) *The first stage is preparation.* Spiritual and organizational groundwork must be laid. For example, prayer and planning must be hand-in-glove. IMPACT leaders must fully understand that administration without inspiration will not accomplish the purposes of the Kingdom—including evangelism, discipleship, and church planting.

Someone once said: "The Army of God moves forward on its knees." It also moves forward on its "sees." It has a vision for the future. If the corporate world plans its work and works its plan, it should be double for the Kingdom. Jesus said, "Suppose one of you wants to build a tower. Will he not first sit down and estimate the cost to see if he has enough money to complete it?" (Luke 14:28).

Advance planning is thoroughly biblical. Old Testament promises and *plans* were fulfilled in the New Testament. God planned a Savior. The Savior planned the outpouring of the Holy Spirit. The Holy Spirit planned the birth of the Church. Everywhere in Scripture you see God planning His work and working His plan.

The second stage is expansion. Once IMPACT is fully in motion, there will be the need for a time-out—a team huddle. This meeting, in a retreat setting, will accomplish three things: (1) the leaders will be refreshed, (2) the game plan will be analyzed, and (3) there will be an emphasis on recruiting—planning the addition of team members.

From that team huddle, energized and focused leaders and team members will be motivated to get back into the game, so to speak. The great work of Kingdom-building will be renewed with new inspiration and focus.

The next stage is consolidation. This will be the point when the harvest is intensified. New missions will be started. New churches will be planted. Pastors will focus on discipling potential leaders. Evangelism plans will be implemented. Leaders and pastors will be trained. The seed sown will begin to bud. And the next stage of the citywide IMPACT will be formed.

Stage four is multiplication. It is the joyful time of the harvest. Those who have gone to the fields to "sow precious seed" will come back "rejoicing." Second-tier church planting will begin to happen. New pastors will be called into the ministry. Church members will start to experience the "I get it!" New leaders will be identified.

It's that precipitation in the prophet's spiritual weather forecast: "I will send you rain in its season, and the ground will yield its crops and the trees of the field their fruit" (Lev. 26:4). Of course, in Kingdom building, success usually means more work. New meeting places will be found. New churches will be opened. New pastors and lay leaders will be recruited and trained. It's not a time for relaxation; it's a time for multiplication. There will be an IMPACT, truly involving members, pastors, and churches in tandem. A coordinated effort will begin to take shape.

STEPS THAT WILL IMPACT YOUR CITY

Planning has both broad strokes and fine strokes. Let's look at some of the fine strokes. What specific actions must you and your team take to impact your community with the gospel? Consider the following, in the four-stage schedule that we have mentioned:

Stage 1: Preparation

Preparation for your IMPACT should begin one year before the launch. The time of preparation is used to focus the hearts of the team and to formulate a strategy for reaching every available person in one city with the gospel of Christ. If that seems like a long preparation time, it's well to remember that Jesus prepared His core disciples *three* years in advance of their ministry.

Luke's introduction to his Gospel indicates the depth and breadth of the disciple's training—both on-site and in the classroom:

> Many have undertaken to draw up an account of the things that have been fulfilled among us, just as they were handed down to us by those who from the first were eyewitnesses and servants of the word. Therefore, since I myself have carefully investigated everything from the beginning, it seemed good also to me to write an orderly account for you, most excellent Theophilus, so that you may know the certainty of the things you have been taught *(Luke 1:1-4).*

Preparation should take place on several important levels:

A. Internal Preparation

1. Preparing the mind. We must prepare ourselves mentally to do something big for God! This is a time to ask some very serious questions:

- If not *here,* then *where* are we going to launch a coordinated effort to reach the lost?
- If not *today,* then *when* are we going to launch a coordinated effort to reach the lost?
- If it is not *me,* then *who* is going to be a part of a coordinated effort to reach the lost?

The harvest is now! Dull or apathetic thinking will not get the job done. Rather, it will take the mental determination of the prophet who faced a godless generation with a game plan: "Here am I, send me!" (Isa. 6:8). The concept of impacting an entire city for Christ must completely saturate our thinking. Before we can impact others, we must be impacted ourselves. We must be prepared mentally.

2. Casting the vision. We must let out the seams of our vision. We must think of how we will motivate others in a great way. Our vision must be enlarged during the year of preparation. Even the transfer of the vision will have a ripple effect: District superintendents will share their vision with pastors, pastors will share their vision with their congregations, and the congregational members will share their vision among themselves. The spirit of movement will be increased. People will look beyond the four walls. They will believe God for great and mighty things.

3. Focusing ministry. During the time of preparation, the focus will be on *multiplication.* For example, pastors will not only think about winning others to Christ and adding them to their church but also think about preparing leaders to start additional churches!

4. Intensifying effort. During IMPACT, ministry speed must be accelerated. It will take our best efforts—during our best time—to accomplish the best results. The time to start ramping up the ministry to meet those demands is during the preparation time. Remember Christ's words, "Do you not say, 'Four months more and then the harvest'? I tell you, open your eyes and look at the fields! They are ripe for harvest'" (John 4:35).

5. Preparing the team. IMPACT will demand increased teams, and increased teams will call for an increased number of leaders. Preparation is the time to prepare not only our own hearts but also the hearts of others to focus their energies and abilities on reaching an entire city.

6. Preparing the church. The local church must rethink its position in the community, rethink its mission and purpose, and be willing to make adjustments in keeping with answers to some important questions:

- What needs to change in order for us to impact a greater number of people? Or, What needs to remain the same in order for us to impact a greater number of people?
- What improvements do we need to make in our methods?
- How is our enthusiasm?
- Are we willing to pay the price for growth?

The core of the church must take a careful look at itself in preparation for impacting its city.

B. External Preparation

External preparations are born during the time of preparation. Organizational flesh is being added to the skeleton of visionary planning.

1. The local church must become acquainted with the city it is going to IMPACT. On a map of the city, it will locate every church, every member, and every potential spot for starting a prayer cell.

2. The local church will also familiarize itself with its own area—with each member's home, each contact home in the area, and each place where the church has an established ministry or activity.

3. The church will use the map in a battle plan. Studying it, the church will begin to strategize the conquering of the city—neighborhood by neighborhood. The church will mark prayer cell locations. It will identify existing Bible-believing and Bible-preaching churches where new converts may be referred. It will also identify areas where a new church may be planted.

C. Strategic Preparation

The specific strategy then begins to take shape.

1. Plan what methods to use in conquering the city, by analyzing examples from other cities.

2. Understand the philosophies and terminologies of the various systems—the Each One Win One, Big Brothers and Big Sisters, and prayer cell systems—so that they may be communicated effectively. For example, when the Big Brothers and Big Sisters plan is spoken of in one place, it should have the same meaning in others. When we speak of the Each One Win One plan in one district, other districts that are developing their IMPACT plan should understand it.

3. A system of growth, using the strategies, must be planned. Each One Win One, Big Brothers and Big Sisters, and prayer cell plans must continue to be utilized—until a movement develops. Each year the strategy progresses to a new level. Each pastor will continue to work to train disciples, and each church will continue to plant new churches. As each plan is continually implemented, it will have its own unique effect on impacting the city.

4. Trained IMPACT coordinators will begin to function on five levels: regional, area, national, district, and local. We will focus on the district and local coordinators and explain their functions and responsibilities.

a. Each district coordinator is selected by the district and works directly with the district superintendent. In the first quarter, he or she will attend the pastors' huddle/retreat. In the second, he or she will be present for the evaluation. In the third, he or she will give guidance for the consecration of the Big Brothers and Big Sisters. In the fourth, he or she will help in the evangelistic campaigns. The coordinator will also be responsible for coordinating all details of IMPACT and work with the pastors to see that they fulfill their work in the local churches.

The district coordinator also keeps a watch on the goal setting and goal reaching. He or she checks on the progress of the prayer cells, missions, and the organization of new churches and the consecration of additional Big Brothers and Big Sisters. He or she will record progress and motivate pastors to reach their goals. (Depending on its size, the district might also need to appoint assistant coordinators.)

b. Each local coordinator is selected by the pastor of a local church to be his or her assistant. He or she should be selected from the pastor's disciples/leadership cell and should be willing to work together as a team with the pastor and the local church. His or her responsibility is to coordinate every part of IMPACT as it relates to the local church. His or her duties will include the following:

- Recording and publicizing the goals set during the pastors' retreat
- Working with the pastor in visiting, evaluating, and encouraging the prayer cells, missions, and new churches
- Working with the district coordinator in organizing the consecration of Big Brothers and Big Sisters in the local church and making sure this service is well publicized and well attended
- Assuring that the plan Each One Win One is used to the greatest extent possible
- Coordinating the celebration services in the prayer cells
- Coordinating the publicity, visitation, and transportation for the citywide evangelistic campaign

It is important to publicize the statistics of advancement from year to year. For example, in the IMPACT to São Paulo there were increases in all areas each year. This undoubtedly contributed to the continued enthusiasm.

D. Spiritual Preparation

It is important to take the city in the name of the Lord. That is why IMPACT is grounded in prayer. Begin organized prayer efforts and continue praying without ceasing. This is done in prayer cells where prayer is offered systematically each week. When the Big Brothers and Big Sisters are consecrated, they pray each day for new converts. Billy Graham once said at a National Prayer Breakfast that the success of any effort may be attributed to three things: "First, prayer; second, prayer; and third, prayer."

During the time of spiritual preparation, thousands of prayers are being offered for specific persons or problems. The planned campaign of prayer also focuses on pastors, coordinators, leaders, and other strategies.

It is systematic prayer that produces a movement on earth. It is exciting to know that the great leaders of evangelistic efforts, such as Dr. Graham, Luis Palau, and Paul Yongi Cho, speak of prayer as the key. IMPACT is not based on money or personalities. That would place limits on what could be done. It is rather based on the *people* of God claiming the *promise* of God: "If my people, who are called by my name, will humble themselves and pray and seek my face . . . then will I hear from heaven . . . and will heal their land" (2 Chron. 7:14).

And it's working—all around the world! People are receiving many blessings from God—and conquering enemy strongholds as well (see Eph. 6:12).

IMPACT is an open declaration of war against Satan. If we look at a city and have the attitude, "We'll just open a little church now and then," or if we are satisfied to maintain a ministry with a handful of members, we do not scare Satan. On the other hand, if we trust God to help us impact entire cities, nations, continents, and the whole world, we cause the enemy a major migraine.

Take caution. Satan will try to stop us! Once we have received our vision from the Lord, we begin to war against the spiritual forces of evil. Consequently, we must continually pray for each other and prepare ourselves spiritually for opposition during this year before beginning the IMPACT.

This first stage of preparation is a time for setting the strategy and plans on which we will build IMPACT. However, with its emphasis on prayer and spiritual growth, it is also a time when the leaders are being filled spiritually. We cannot give if we are empty. First, we must be filled. This includes pastors, superintendents, missionaries, and members of the church. Later, we will impact the city that God has placed before us.

Stage 2: Expansion

This is the stage of IMPACT, the year of evangelistic adventure, when we begin to fight the great battle. There are four basic activities (one each quarter) in this year of expansion that the district superintendent and district coordinator will supervise.

A. The Retreat (First Quarter)

1. In this retreat, we will inform and inspire the pastors with the philosophy of IMPACT. The details of the plans will be reviewed and questions answered. We must be informed and also motivated.

2. We will evaluate our present situation. It will be necessary to see where we are, what we have done—and what we haven't done. We will look at where we have made mistakes, where we can improve, and what we can learn from the experiences in other cities.

3. We may have to change the direction of the ministerial mentality. Negative attitudes must be confronted and eliminated. This is a time to develop a mentality of conquest.

4. We will take a vote during the retreat to see if we are willing to take on this task. Not all pastors are enthusiastic at the beginning. In every city, there are many pastors who are interested and want to be involved. Others may only observe. Some may be negative. However, as the IMPACT progresses in the city, those who were observers in the beginning become involved the following year.

The same holds true for those who are negative. History has proven that some eventually ask forgiveness for not participating. They then get involved by starting prayer cells and raising leaders to reach their communities for Christ.

5. We will determine a ministry strategy. Each pastor will project his or her church's action for the year. Special emphasis will be placed on how leaders will be developed during the following months.

6. We will set a faith goal that will target how many prayer cells will be formed, how many missions will be started, and how many new churches will be organized during the year. The pastor also projects, by faith, how many disciples will be trained to care for the prayer cells, missions, and daughter churches.

7. The district superintendent will introduce the team—the district coordinator and assistants (if appointed), who were previously selected. Special prayer will be offered for them and for the IMPACT.

B. An Evaluation of the Prayer Cells (Second Quarter)

1. In this quarter, a meeting will be held to evaluate the cells in each local church. Note: If a city has more than four churches, ministry areas should be determined by dividing the city into sections. The churches in each section will coordinate their efforts to impact that section for Christ. During the second quarter, churches in each section will have a meeting, which will include the district superintendent, the pastors, the district and local church coordinators, and other team members. If there is more than one section in a city, these meetings can be on consecutive days.

The meeting will include several actions:
- There will be a review of how prayer cells function and a time for discussion.
- Each pastor will display the map of cells and missions that have opened.
- The leaders of the cells and missions will be introduced.
- A review of answered prayers from the prayer cell notebooks may also be included.
- There will also be a time for testimonies.

2. A seminar (including the leader cell/disciples) on IMPACT should be held on the Saturday following the section evaluation meetings. In this seminar, a report of the retreat is given.

3. The same Saturday, following the seminar, members of the participating churches are invited to a service of celebration, consecration, and revival. A map will be presented, showing section by section where projected prayer cells and missions will be located. The service will inform the entire district of the plans to conquer the city.

The service will also motivate additional members to become leaders in the task of opening new prayer cells or missions. Others will offer to open their homes. The disciples are already beginning to multiply. The service will conclude with the district coordinator giving a challenging message and announcing the date for the consecration of Big Brothers and Big Sisters during the following quarter.

C. The Consecration of Big Brothers and Big Sisters (Third Quarter)

On a date agreed upon with the district coordinator, there will be a consecration service for new Big Brothers and Big Sisters in each participating local church. Prior to the service, the district coordinator will instruct and supervise the local coordinator in implementing the plan.

The district coordinator will direct the service:

1. The district coordinator will have materials regarding the Big Brothers and Big Sisters plan distributed.

2. The district coordinator will see that the Big Brothers and Big Sisters are given instruction to begin praying for their list of 10 unconverted persons.

3. As an encouragement to the attendees and the participants, the district coordinator will present the statistics on the number of Big Brothers and Big Sisters participants, the number of prayer cells started—along with examples of answered prayers, the number of leaders trained, the number of missions opened, and the number of daughter churches organized.

D. Evangelistic Campaigns (Fourth Quarter)

Throughout the year, spiritual preparations for the evangelistic campaigns have been made through organized prayer efforts in the prayer cells and the missions.

1. Evangelistic campaigns will be held on three levels:
   - Level one is a celebration service held on a weekday during the first week and is usually located in the church or building that the campaign will take place.
   - Level two is a local church evangelistic campaign held during the second week. The celebration services function as satellite campaigns of the local churches by bringing the new contacts to the church's campaign.
   - Level three is a citywide evangelistic campaign, held during the third week. The citywide evangelistic campaign is the culmination of the cycle of special campaigns. It will be well organized, well publicized, and include plans for transporting Big Brothers and Big Sisters and the unconverted members on their prayer list to the campaign. Those who have already been converted during local church campaigns will also attend.

2. On the last day/night of the evangelistic campaign, the district coordinator will give special recognition to the team that has been working on the IMPACT campaign during the year: the evangelist, leaders of prayer cells, Big Brothers and Big Sisters, counselors, pastors, committee members, and so on.

3. There should also be an announcement concerning new prayer cells and Big Brothers and Big Sisters plans for the following year. The Big Brothers and Big Sisters are reminded to begin discipling the new converts and to help them prepare for baptism. That will prevent an empty space between this campaign and the next.

During the 12 months of the second year, four special activities will be repeated: (1) the retreat, (2) an evaluation of the prayer cells, (3) the consecration of additional Big Brothers and Big Sisters, and (4) an evangelistic campaign.

The four activities emphasize the important areas of IMPACT: personal discipleship, ministry in homes, personal evangelism, and mass evangelism. Once implemented in a citywide effort, the city has been impacted. And local churches will be enthused to begin the cycle once again.

Stage 3: Consolidation

In the third stage of IMPACT, the efforts of evangelism and discipleship in the local churches and districts are consolidated.

1. New churches will be organized from missions. Many prayer cell leaders have been called and trained as preachers, while some are in the Theological Education by Extension program preparing to lead a mission or church.

2. Evangelism and discipleship efforts will be expanded. Not only will the harvest of the two previous years be organized into vibrant ministries, but also there will be a concerted effort to reach more people with the gospel in the coming year. The success of the previous campaigns will motivate Christians for the next.

   a. There will be continued growth—and a multiplication of churches.

   b. The evangelism and discipleship plans will be repeated with even more experience and enthusiasm.

   c. The experiences of the previous two to three years will reveal proven criteria for evaluating campaign goals and effectiveness, including some invaluable questions:

   - Are we really conquering the city?
   - What are the visible results?
   - Do we have organizational limitations?
   - Are new Christians being mainstreamed into local churches?
   - Are new leaders being developed?
   - How are new pastors being recruited and trained?
   - Where should we be planting new missions and churches?

Christians who implemented IMPACT in South America had an interesting look back. In the previous 30 years of their existence, only 5 new churches had been organized. But during the three years of their IMPACT, 25 new churches were organized. Previously it took one district 30 years to win 346 persons to Christ, but during its three-year IMPACT, 700 more had been won! Their total membership grew to 1,046. Evaluation was one of the important steps in their success.

Stage 4: Multiplication

Evaluation by the churches in South America also revealed how the churches were multiplying themselves. For example, when they began their fourth year, they were surprised to find that all areas of their IMPACT were multiplying. During the first year of IMPACT in São Paulo, for instance, there was 1 mother church and 5 daughter churches. In the second year, there were 2 mother churches and *7* daughter churches. The third year revealed *7* mother churches and *13* daughter churches!

That's the miracle of multiplication. Impact produces results! As each level of growth is realized, there is an even greater motivation to reach the next—and to expand the area of influence. When God's people commit themselves to working in tandem to conquer their city, they are on the way to conquering their region—and, soon, their entire nation. What's next? The world. All for the glory of God!

V.
LEADERSHIP

⑩ GOALS AND LEADERSHIP

We know what we want to do. We want to motivate Christians in local churches and districts to reach their community, their region, and their country for Christ. And we know how we can do it. In the power of the Holy Spirit, we can utilize the best of the New Testament church's methods for aggressive church multiplication. To do that, we will also want to model the best of that church's personal and corporate disciplines—especially in the area of church leadership.

The apostle Paul was one of the Early Church's greatest leaders. Many factors lead us to make that judgment, including several defining descriptions in God's Word:

- *First, he had a passion for Christ.*

    Whatever was to my profit I now consider loss for the sake of Christ. What is more, I consider everything a loss compared to the surpassing greatness of knowing Christ Jesus my Lord, for whose sake I have lost all things. I consider them rubbish, that I may gain Christ and be found in him, not having a righteousness of my own that comes from the law, but that which is through faith in Christ—the righteousness that comes from God and is by faith. I want to know Christ and the power of his resurrection and the fellowship of sharing in his sufferings, becoming like him in his death, and so, somehow, to attain to the resurrection from the dead *(Phil. 3:7-11)*.

- *Second, he was passionate about winning souls.*

    When I preach the gospel, I cannot boast, for I am compelled to preach. Woe to me if I do not preach the gospel! If I preach voluntarily, I have a reward; if not voluntarily, I am simply discharging the trust committed to me. What then is my reward? Just this: that in preaching the gospel I may offer it free of charge, and so not make use of my rights in preaching it. Though I am free and belong to no man, I make myself a slave to everyone, to win as many as possible. To the Jews I became like a Jew, to win the Jews. To those under the law I became like one under the law (though I myself am not under the law), so as to win those under the law. To those not having the law I became like one not having the law (though I am not free from God's law but am under Christ's law), so as to win those not having the law. To the weak I became weak, to win the weak. I have become all things to all men so that by all possible means I might save some *(1 Cor. 9:16-22)*.

- *Third, he was passionate about doing things the right way.*

    Our people must learn to devote themselves to doing what is good, in order that they may provide for daily necessities and not live unproductive lives *(Titus 3:14)*.

- *Fourth, he was passionate about setting a course of action for his life and ministry.*

    Not that I have already obtained all this, or have already been made perfect, but I press on to take hold of that for which Christ Jesus took hold of me. Brothers, I do not consider myself yet to have taken hold of it. But one thing I do: Forgetting what is behind and straining toward what is ahead, I press on toward the goal to win the prize for which God has called me heavenward in Christ Jesus. All of us who are mature should take such a view of things. And if on some point you think differently, that too God will make clear to you. Only let us live up to what we have already attained *(Phil. 3:12-16)*.

VISION

Paul's unique success in reaching masses of people with the gospel lay in his ability to look through the binoculars of long-range planning. He visualized the direction of his ministry, and his vision directly influenced his leadership. Any effort for reaching a greater number of people must first have a clear purpose and then a definite program. The leader and the group behind the effort must determine where they want to go. And that takes vision.

Vision is different from a goal because it requires the ability to see what steps (goals) should be taken and then determines how to take them. Vision sees the results of a program even before it is launched. In our case, it means seeing a harvest of new believers and the planting of new churches before the first plan is implemented.

Thus the leader must (1) be open to God's guidance, (2) be able to capture that guidance and communicate it to others, and then (3) encourage them to help make it happen. To do that, the leader must organize people to reap a harvest and achieve New Testament growth in church ministry.

Setting Goals for the Vision

Goals are the signposts that lead us toward the fulfillment of our vision. Goal setting is linking a plan with a dream. Without goals, we have no way of achieving our vision. Paul said, "I do not run like a man running aimlessly" (1 Cor. 9:26). It is a philosophy that every Christian leader should model. We aim at our *vision,* and as we reach our *goals,* we run toward it.

Guidelines for Setting Goals

Goals may originate in heaven, but they are set on the earth. Whether personal or corporate, goal setting is the lifeblood of successful ventures—Kingdom or otherwise. For the most part, success isn't accidental. It is the result of definite direction and diligent efforts. For example, you don't just arrive at a destination. First, you go *in the direction* of that destination, plan your route, map the course, and then *diligently* follow the map. Goal setting is mapping the course. There are several important principles to follow:

1. Goals Should Be Written Out

It has been said that only 3 percent of persons record their goals on paper. Most people do not write out their goals because they do not think goals are important. The time and effort you take in planning and organizing your goals on paper or in an electronic file is invaluable to your personal life or to your organization.

2. Goals Should Be Promoted

When it comes to setting corporate goals for your organization, it is not enough to list them. They should be publicized. Secret goals will not enable a group to follow a leader. It must know where the leader is going.

They may be promoted in practical ways. For example, in Church of the Nazarene world missions, field directors meet with each leader of ministries under their supervision (theological education, church growth and evangelism, pastoral ministries, and so on) to set goals for the coming year. The goals are listed and analyzed carefully to see if they are viable. Then they are publicly announced.

Granted, some leaders have "goal-a-phobia." They don't list/promote goals because they are afraid they will not reach them and will suffer personal embarrassment as a result. But the best understanding of Christian leadership is based on the principles of the Word of God. And the Word of God challenges leaders to be goal-setters.

For example, God listed goals for His creation. "He is patient with you, not wanting anyone to perish, but everyone to come to repentance" (2 Pet. 3:9). He "wants all men to be saved and to come to a knowledge of the truth" (1 Tim. 2:4). God's purpose is the salvation of the world. He not only listed goals for achieving that purpose but also passionately set the course for accomplishing it (John 3:16).

3. Goals Should Be Definite and Measurable

It's not enough to say, "I want the church to grow," or "We plan to have a good year." We must be willing to go out on the limb spiritually and numerically to set a definite and measurable goal: "We plan to gain 100 new members in the coming year." Or "I am going to train five new mission leaders this year." Or "We plan to start a new church in (a specific place) by (a certain date)."

4. Goals Should Be Evaluated

Goals need a periodic inspection. It is a good practice to examine goals that have been set in previous years to see whether they have been reached. Often you will discover ways in which God has miraculously rewarded your goal-setting faith. Goals reached are victories won! And victories won motivate people to even greater achievement.

An evaluation of goals can also help you make midcourse corrections. An honest evaluation of unrealistic goals will often help you set a revised and more practical course. For example, the apostle Peter's goal of unwavering loyalty to the Master was reevaluated after the fireside fiasco during Jesus' trial. Your midcourse evaluation and correction will certainly not be as catastrophic. Nevertheless, an honest appraisal of the direction you are heading will not only keep you on track but also help you choose a new and better track.

5. Goals Should Be Set in Faith

Sadly, many Christian leaders are insecure about their own abilities, and this influences their organization's ability to accomplish its goals. As a result, they are not willing to take risks. They are afraid to dream. They don't set goals because they don't have the vision or faith to believe that God will use them to carry out *big plans*. Goals should be set in the concrete of God's promises and power.

For example, at one point in the South American Church of the Nazarene's history there were 503 churches. The leaders set a goal of planting 1,000 churches within 10 years. God honored their faith. They not only reached their goal of organizing church No. 1,000 but also did it nearly 5 years ahead of schedule!

What you see is what you get. If leaders aim at a goal of zero, they'll usually reach it. That's one reason why many pastors and churches are in a maintenance mode instead of a growth mode. The Great Commission isn't a principle of maintenance. It is a principle of aggressive multiplication. And it isn't being fully carried out unless *everyone everywhere* is doing *everything* possible to reach *every person* with the gospel of Christ.

6. Goals Should Be Guided by the Holy Spirit

Seminary professor Dr. Paul Orjala once wept as he told his class that God took a great risk when He put His mission in the hands of humans. Humans are often insecure, unstable, and selfish. However, God provided a remedy during a clinic in the Upper Room. On the Day of Pentecost, the Holy Spirit baptized the disciples. They would never be the same.

On that day, He filled the disciples with His Holy Spirit—uniting His heart with theirs. Not only that, He replaced their selfishness with a spirit of service. In place of their insecurity, He filled them with power. Instead of instability, they now had a life-changing spiritual purpose. The baptism of the Holy Spirit is still the solution.

Our goal setting must be Spirit-led. It must not focus on our achievements but on the accomplishments and provisions of Calvary. Our message about the power and purity of intention that a believer receives when he or she is filled with the Holy Spirit must permeate our goals. Our goals must bring honor and glory to the Lord Jesus Christ.

Reaching Goals

Reaching personal and corporate goals is even more exciting than setting them. Israel understood that when they commemorated their victory over the Philistines: "The men of Israel rushed out of Mizpah and pursued the Philistines, slaughtering them along the way to a point below Beth Car. Then Samuel took a stone and set it up between Mizpah and Shen. He named it Ebenezer, saying, 'Thus far has the LORD helped us'" (1 Sam. 7:11-12). The Ebenezer stone was a milestone—a goal reached. The victory party was a culmination of the direction in which the prophet had led the armies, the communication of the battle plan, and the dependence upon God's provisions.

Goal setting isn't rocket science (unless you're a rocket scientist). It is simply detailing points at which the vision has been partially accomplished. There are some further guidelines in setting goals for impacting a city, region, or country for Christ.

1. Goals Should Be Reachable

One district superintendent set a goal of doubling the number of churches in his district in one year. However, he admitted he never intended for his district to reach that goal. His idea was that if he reached *half* of the goal he had set, it would be good enough. There is a leadership fallout in such a plan.

Leading by misleading is never a good idea. People lose confidence in the credibility of a leader who cannot set realistic and reachable goals. It is important that you know how you intend to reach your goals when you plan them.

For example, when the goal of organizing 50 churches in 10 years in the Dominican Republic was set, the denominational leaders first had an idea of how they were going to reach it. They had a plan to mobilize the Dominican people to reach what seemed to be an unreachable goal. Church leaders began to meet monthly with the pastors to talk and pray about it. When they shared the plan, people began to believe it could be reached, and it was!

2. Goals Should Have Long-Range and Short-Range Dimensions

Goals have different levels of impact. Long-range goals are important but often must have a short-range plan for reaching them. Difficult circumstances may come along to block the road to long-range success. Short-range goals are then set to overcome the roadblocks. By organizing and reorganizing short-range goals, it is possible to return to—and reach—the original long-range goal. This means we will often set short-range goals for each day. To reach a long-range goal, we must form habits that will move us daily toward the goal.

3. Goal "Barriers" Should Be Dealt With

As long as the raw material of church growth is people, there will be people problems. And since building new churches depends on organizational bureaucracy, there will be an occasional bureaucracy problem. An important ability of a leader is to find solutions for such barriers. A person of vision must overcome problems to reach goals. How?

First, act as if they will happen. Anticipate them in your thinking. Every venture will have its eventual barriers. As you plan your personal or corporate actions, anticipate some opposition. Jesus promised that in the world we would have trouble!

Second, act prayerfully. The grand old gospel song advises, "Take your burden to the Lord and leave it there." Seek first the counsel of the Lord before seeking the counsel of others. Seek the counsel of the Word. Spend time with Dr. Jesus in discussing a remedy. The wisdom that comes from a season of prayer will usually help you deal with a winter of discontent.

Third, act quickly. Once you have the mind of the Lord and are in fellowship with His Spirit, move in His direction. A delay in dealing with a personal or organizational problem will only exacerbate the problem. Time doesn't heal all wounds. Often, it makes them worse.

Four, act like Jesus. The best way to handle a human crisis is with a heavenly spirit. A proud or arrogant attitude will only add height to barriers. An apology may be the best short-range plan to solve a longer-range problem. Understanding the hurts of someone standing guard over your barrier will go a long way in helping to build a bridge to that person.

4. Motivation Should Be Used to Reach Goals

Lofty goals and lowered expectations are a dangerous ministry mix. The Early Church didn't need motivation. They were only years away from the Resurrection. The Savior's mission was being fulfilled daily in the lives of His followers. Pentecost had set a three-alarm fire in the heart of the Church.

But obviously, times have changed the Church. Resurrection and Pentecost have commonly been relegated to tiny boxes on the pages of the calendar. Christians who should be focusing on world evangelization are, instead, focusing on making ends meet—while keeping both ends of the candle burning.

Obviously, some intense motivation is in order. History proves it can be done. One church leader told of a pastor who had resigned, stating that he could not make his church grow. A young pastor who had been converted less than a year before was appointed to that same church. Highly motivated and full of faith that the church *could* grow, the new pastor received 30 new members into the church during the first three months of his ministry!

What motivates Christians to reach evangelism and discipleship goals? There are several factors:

First, biblical preaching. "Thus says the Lord" has a far greater impact than "Thus says the preacher." Biblical preaching is an important tool for motivating God's people. It not only builds spiritual faith but also provides a firm foundation for the purpose and ministries of the church.

Second, promotion. Goals shouldn't be the church's best-kept secret. For example, church growth programs—including the accompanying goals—must not be kept in the closet. They should be kept on the front burner. The more we promote a plan in public, the more persons will begin to believe that it is important. Also, constant promotion will help turn a negative church atmosphere into a positive church.

Promoting goal setting, and recognizing goal reaching, teaches personal discipline. Denominational leaders themselves should focus on promoting church growth goal setting and goal reaching. That is why they continue to produce materials (such as the posters for Each One Win One plans, or forms for the Big Brothers and Big Sisters plan). That is why this book was written. That is why instructional manuals are written and printed. That is why various media are produced. Promotion creates an energy that the Holy Spirit can inspire to reach the lost and train the believer.

Third, incentives. Let's face it. Citizens of the 21st century are bonus oriented. This is the frequent flyer miles generation—a generation raised to expect rewards and add-ons. Yet, there isn't usually room in the budget for luxury cruises or Rolex watch prizes. But creative leaders can provide some of their own incentives. Special recognition from the pulpit or in the church publications can provide exposure and recognition. Perhaps you could take individuals to lunch or dinner and let them know how much you appreciate their work. Plaques or trophies and news releases with pictures included in the local paper are excellent ways to recognize committed people. There are many ways to help Christian workers develop a positive attitude and to be motivated in reaching goals.

Fourth, recognition. When goals are reached, there should be a celebration. Victory parties motivate people toward additional victories. Recognition of goal reaching should be a big deal. Nothing lets the air out of the ministry balloon any more than letting a milestone pass without recognizing it. Come to think of it, the Church itself is heading toward a final honors banquet—the Marriage Supper of the Lamb.

Fifth, example. People are motivated by the persistent efforts of others. When Christian leaders do their own personal best in reaching goals, Christian followers will be motivated to do the same. Paul suggested that when he encouraged his disciples to follow him as he followed Christ (1 Cor. 11:1). Lazy or lax leaders usually raise a company of lazy or lax followers. On the contrary, leaders who are personally motivated—and diligently work toward reaching public goals—attract a cadre of workers who will seek to do their personal best.

It takes persistence to reach goals. We must do everything in our power to reach them. Excuses, problems, or barriers must not stop us. Even failures must be used to gain success. That is the commitment of a true leader. And leaders are the key to impacting the world for Christ.

THE LEADER AND THE TEAM

The Church was launched in that team huddle on the Day of Pentecost. But it wasn't the first team meeting. Jesus built His strategy for world evangelization around the team concept. He chose a team of 12 disciples, invested three years of His life on earth with them, encouraged them to add additional team members, and then sent them out to reach the world. Obviously it worked! It is inconceivable that Christian leaders would use any different method in these days. Though some have tried, by appointing themselves as a committee of one to carry out the mission and purpose of Christ, they usually end tired and fruitless.

Christ's way of teamwork is the best way. Let's look at it, in light of impacting a church, district, region, or country for Christ.

Form the Team

Theodore Roosevelt once said, "The best executive is the one that has enough common sense to select good men to do what he wants to do, and to stay out of their way while they do it." A leader should be aware that he cannot implement the vision of God alone. For that reason, teamwork is the best approach. Jesus used it. "Jesus went out to a mountainside to pray, and spent the night praying to God. When morning came, he called his disciples to him and chose twelve of them, whom he also designated apostles" (Luke 6:12-13).

Jesus Christ could have implemented the vision of God by himself. In one sense, He did. He accomplished redemption by His sinless life and His sacrificial death on the Cross. He also recruited, trained, and commissioned a team—the 12 apostles—to carry out the plans of His Heavenly Father, to teach and preach a message of love and forgiveness that included those who lived under the bondage of Old Testament laws and regulations. Both the teamwork and the message are living examples of their potential.

In Brazil, Bruno Radi had a vision for reaching the entire area with the gospel. That vision included the development of a team to accomplish the mission. This is what happened: Over 100 churches were planted, and more than 4,000 members were added to the Church—in just eight years. In addition, leaders from all over the region—and around the world—caught the vision of forming a team, and the success of their teamwork has influenced church planting around the globe!

Supervise the Team

A leader does not control the team. A leader supervises/guides the team in reaching goals that have been established by leadership and agreed upon. This was the strategy of the Lord Jesus. He said, "I tell you the truth: It is for your good that I am going away. Unless I go away, the Counselor will not come to you; but if I go, I will send him to you" (John 16:7). The spiritual supervision of the Holy Spirit through the team/disciples ministry would be hearts-on instead of hands-on. Jesus would soon ascend into heaven. However, the supervision of the team would remain through the guidance of His Spirit.

A denominational leader may set the agenda for evangelism and discipleship ministries in a region, but it is the team that carries it out. District leaders and local church pastors make ministry decisions and plant churches. And laypersons win people to Christ by personal evangelism or bringing them into an evangelistic environment. It is truly a team effort.

Since they have freedom to make individual plans that relate to the agenda, the team has developed a strong sense of ownership. The leader's task is to guide, not control; to supervise the work, not the people.

Motivate the Team

A leader is a motivator, not just a manager. A manager or administrator is seen as one who looks after the details of the team's work. However, a leader is one who motivates the team with enthusiasm and inspiration. A motivated team achieves a much higher level of production. The leader is a catalyst. Without a catalyst, a reaction does not occur. All the elements may be present to create a reaction, but the catalyst makes it happen.

It is like having thousands of molecules of oxygen and hydrogen in a container. They need the catalyst of electricity to produce a reaction that results in water. Likewise, God has given the elements that we need for a successful reaction. Leaders are catalysts that stimulate the church to grow.

As we've mentioned, Paul was a catalytic leader who extended the Church throughout the known world. He said to his disciples, "Join with others in following my example, brothers, and take note of those who live according to the pattern we gave you" (Phil. 3:17). Paul wasn't pretentious or self-centered. He was simply inspiring and motivating others in the same way his Master had motivated and inspired him. What is the game plan for motivating the team? There are some important motivators.

1. Enthusiasm

Enthusiasm energizes and challenges people to action. Enthusiasm is what gives life to an organization. The *organization* becomes an *organism* when it has a leader who gives it motivation, enthusiasm, and life and who gets excited about reaching for the prize. We need leaders who are ready and willing to give the credit away and give a pat on the back to those who are striving to reach the goals.

2. Relationship

A leader must spend time with his or her people. Quality time with the team in prayer, worship, or discussion of goals will pay off in quality effort. Fellow workers must know that they are just that—fellow workers. By making an investment of friendship and relating to the team in a humble and human way, the team is motivated to do their best.

3. Reporting

Team members should know they will give an account of their efforts. Jesus said that one day we will even give an account of our conversation: "I tell you that men will have to give account on the day of judgment for every careless word they have spoken" (Matt. 12:36). Reporting times are important in dealing with faulty directions or actions. Also, they reinforce the team member's ability—and accountability. Reporting times also give the leader an opportunity to evaluate goals, make corrections, and keep the team on course. In other words, they are times when the *catalyst* comes together with the *elements*. The *reaction* produces motivated workers who press on to achieve their goals.

4. Encouraging

Discouragement is a stop that everyone in ministry will make on the road to success. No matter how much speed you've built up, around one bend or another, there will be a roadblock set up by the master discourager, Satan. His intent is to suck the very life out of your every action and turn it into a reaction!

But discouragement is a precious moment for the Christian leader. It's a time to put in a good word to the team member. It's a time for the leader to reinforce the confidence he or she has in the team member, a time to reinforce gifts and relationship, a time for prayer, a time for lifting—a time to encourage.

Encouragement is one of the greatest team motivators.

5. Freedom

It's hard to double a volunteer's pay! *Volunteer* suggests that time given to a ministry effort is just that—given. So, volunteer ministry team members should not only be respected for their contribution but also be given some latitude in their actions. Leaders aren't pushers. They guide from out in front. Certainly, leadership suggests that someone be in the lead. However, if there aren't any followers, the title is meaningless.

Leaders do have a plan—one that inspires others to follow. Leaders lead as much by their example as they do by their manuals. The leader casts the vision and sets the goals, then lets the team members develop ownership and integrate them into their specific situation.

WHERE DO WE GO FROM HERE?

We've examined the plans.

We've cast a vision.

We've set some reachable goals.

Now what? The enemy of our faith would want us to do nothing. He would want us to just tread water, to keep talking about the need to motivate Christians to evangelism and discipleship, instead of acting on it. Procrastination is the great enemy of evangelism. We must fight it with all of our might! How do we start doing the things that need to be done?

1. Pray

Get away from the office, turn off the cell phone, and ask the receptionist to take messages. Spend some time with the greatest soul winner of all—Jesus. Ask Him to stir up your heart, to take you out of your comfort zone. Ask Him to give you a view of the harvest field through the window of His heart. Pray about the harvest and gather an army of prayer warriors who will storm the gates of heaven with the requests of earth.

2. Practice

Be a soul winner yourself. Ask the Lord to, in the words of the song, "lay some soul upon my heart, and love that soul through me." The greatest evangelism and discipleship effort your church or your district will ever see can start with you. Begin to pray about someone in your church or community who needs the Lord. Will you make plans to present the gospel to that person? Remember, everyone you make eye contact with is so valuable to God that He sent His only Son to die for him or her. Will you make the effort to lead that person to the Savior? Will you teach that person how to grow in faith and become a soul winner?

3. Plan

Plan to reach beyond the four walls of your organization. You may start small, but a small start is better than no start! Start dreaming. Then start putting plans to your dream (set goals). Begin to form your team for reaching the lost through your own church. And then make plans to be part of a wider effort. Make an IMPACT—work in tandem with other church leaders to reach your community for Christ.

4. Project

Break out of the barriers! Dream big! Plan big! Gather your resources and go for the gold! Tear down the walls that separate you or your organization from a dying world that needs a Savior. God has called you to build His Church—through His people. Create a system that produces a movement. A movement will result in the growth of the Church, the multiplication of believers, new churches, and persons called to the ministry.

Start a movement—not just a ministry—a movement that is committed to Each One Win One, that recruits spiritual Big Brothers and Big Sisters to evangelize and disciple, that turns prayer cells into missions, and missions into new churches.

Set high goals, and make the church a force for good and for God. Inspire others through biblical preaching. Call the church to prayer. Covenant to build a church that moves the church toward God.

Be a leader who is willing to sacrifice. Be a leader who longs for the fire of Pentecost—who is willing to be set aflame and then to be used to spread the fire! Be a leader who is willing to stake everything you are, everything you have, and everything you hope to be on the eternal promise of God's Word: "Now to him who is able to do immeasurably more than all we ask or imagine, according to his power that is at work within us, to him be glory in the church and in Christ Jesus throughout all generations, for ever and ever! Amen" (Eph. 3:20-21).

APPENDIXES

Note: The authors thank the Lake View Park Church of the Nazarene in Oklahoma City for applying the principles of Each One Win One and allowing us to use the following pages as examples.

Louie Bustle
Stan Toler

APPENDIX A
LEADER'S GUIDES

THE SOUTH AMERICAN STRATEGY

I. A New Mentality
    A. Developing spiritual communities
        1. Spiritual commitment resulted in numerical <u>growth</u> (Acts 16:5).
        2. Be willing to use a new <u>plan</u> to reach as many as possible (1 Cor. 9:12-23).
    B. Back to the New Testament
        1. Employ <u>new</u> methods.
        2. Move from exclusive to <u>inclusive</u> (Acts 10:34).

II. A Plan of Mobilization: Each One Win One
    A. Total <u>participation</u> becomes a priority.
    B. The challenge to win <u>one</u>.

III. The Power of Our Witness
    A. Growth begins with <u>enthused</u> believers.
        1. <u>Personal</u> relationships influence the lost.
        2. The gospel <u>chain</u> begins by reaching one person.
    B. The key to evangelism is not programming but <u>participation</u>.
        1. Many <u>people</u> have a desire for someone to love them.
        2. What happens when the whole <u>church</u> expresses love and interest?

IV. An Emphasis on Natural Growth
    A. The natural growth of the <u>church</u>.
        1. It must have a heart that is <u>rich</u> in ministry (2 Cor. 8:1-5).
        2. The church doesn't grow because of its <u>resources</u>; rather it grows because of its Source (Zech. 4:6).
    B. <u>Aggressive</u> church multiplication does not depend on outside resources.
        1. We must have a deep concern for the <u>lost</u>.
        2. We must be willing to give of our <u>personal</u> resources.

V. The Infilling of the Holy Spirit
    A. The <u>clarion</u> call
        1. Every believer must be <u>filled</u> with the Holy Spirit.
        2. The power to <u>witness</u>.
    B. <u>Preach</u> this message
        1. With <u>confidence</u>!
        2. With <u>passion</u>!

VI. A Spirit of Giving
    Raising the level of <u>vision</u>
        1. There must be a commitment to <u>building</u> the kingdom of God.
        2. Aggressive church multiplication begins with a spirit of <u>giving</u>.

VII. The Power of the Team
    A. Team <u>spirit</u> includes
        1. A <u>willingness</u> to share
        2. Joining <u>hands</u>
    B. Developing an evangelistic <u>network</u>

1. <u>House</u> churches
2. Citywide <u>campaigns</u>

VIII. Empowering the Laity
    A. Total <u>mobilization</u> of the laity
        1. Guidance through <u>inspiration</u>
        2. <u>Leader</u>-inspired initiatives
    B. The expectation to <u>plant</u> new churches
        1. Go and make <u>disciples</u>.
        2. Rapid <u>growth</u> demands the laity to be mobilized.

IX. The Call to Take Up the Cross
    The emphasis on <u>sacrifice</u>
        1. <u>Joyful</u> suffering (Acts 5:17-42)
        2. Dedicated <u>devotion</u>

X. Decentralizing Theological Education
    Education by <u>Extension</u>
        1. Taking the <u>seminary</u> to the people
        2. A <u>constant</u> resource of trained pastors

A BIBLICAL AND HISTORICAL STRATEGY

Intro.: Accelerated Church Multiplication

    A. How the Holy Spirit worked in <u>Acts</u>

        1. The Church <u>multiplied</u> (Acts 4:4).

        2. The Church <u>united</u> (Acts 6:7).

        3. The Church <u>grew</u> (Acts 9:31).

        4. The Church's <u>influence</u> was far-reaching (Acts 11:21).

        5. The Church was <u>Scripture-honoring</u> (Acts 12:24).

    B. Paul's <u>mission</u>

        1. To point people to <u>Christ</u>

        2. To <u>disciple</u> new believers

        3. To <u>train</u> for leadership

  I. Strategies That Impact the World

    A. Aggressive <u>church</u> multiplication

        1. Catching the <u>vision</u>

        2. <u>Impacting</u> our world

    B. The <u>strategy</u>

        1. Impact <u>individuals</u>

        2. Impact <u>neighborhoods</u>

        3. Impact <u>communities</u>

        4. Impact <u>cities</u>

        5. Impact <u>regions</u> and countries

 II. By the Book

    Intro.: Our strategy is <u>based</u> on the Word of God

        1. The <u>promise</u> of the Holy Spirit's power (Acts 1:8)

        2. The promise of the Holy Spirit's <u>guidance</u> (John 16:13)

    A. The Example of Moses (Exod. 18)

        1. The <u>biblical</u> account

        2. The <u>results</u>

    B. The Need for External Leadership

        1. Taking the message to the <u>streets</u>

        2. <u>Go</u> and make disciples (Matt. 28:19)

    C. The Example of Paul

        1. Paul's aim was not only to grow churches but also to grow <u>leaders</u>.

        2. His <u>priority</u>—to exalt Christ.

        3. His <u>plan</u>—to mentor others.

        4. His method—to <u>develop</u> additional leaders.

    D. The Best Leader of All—Jesus

        1. Jesus' leadership <u>stands</u> alone.

            a. He <u>impacted</u> the world.

            b. He employed external <u>leadership</u>.

            c. His <u>strategy</u> was successful.

        2. Jesus still calls His Church to follow Him.

           Operating at <u>four</u> important levels

            a. Level One—<u>individuals</u>

      b. Level Two—<u>leaders</u>

      c. Level Three—<u>daughter</u> churches

      d. Level Four—<u>mother</u> churches

III. Overcoming Church Problems

    A. It overcomes by <u>going</u>.

    B. It overcomes by <u>recruiting</u>.

    C. It overcomes by <u>equipping</u>.

IV. The Potential

    A. Believers have incredible <u>potential</u>.

    B. Believers can <u>impact</u> their world.

 V. Follow the Leaders

    A. It's up to <u>you</u>!

    B. Be a part of a movement that <u>impacts</u> your world.

THE JESUS STRATEGY

Intro.: The Life and Ministry of Jesus

    A. It changed <u>lives</u>.

    B. It changed <u>history</u>.

  I. Jesus Depended on His Father (John 12:49).

    A. He depended on His Father for His <u>life</u> and ministry.

    B. Jesus began and ended His ministry by <u>praying</u> to His Father (Matt. 4; Luke 22:42).

    C. Jesus prayed for His <u>disciples</u> (John 17:1-21).

        1. He <u>reaffirmed</u> His ministry purpose.

        2. He communicated His <u>intent</u>.

        3. He <u>encouraged</u> His disciples.

        4. He <u>revealed</u> His strategy.

  II. Jesus Had an Evangelistic Purpose (Luke 19:10).

    A. He was <u>focused</u> on the main thing.

    B. He was <u>never</u> sidetracked.

    C. He coordinated His <u>efforts</u>.

  III. Jesus Wisely Selected His Disciples (Matt. 10).

    A. He found workers and put them to <u>greater</u> work.

    B. He <u>carefully</u> chose His disciples.

  IV. He Motivated His Disciples (Luke 10:22-24).

    A. After selecting His disciples, He <u>motivated</u> them.

    B. He spent <u>time</u> with His disciples.

    C. He took great <u>interest</u> in His disciples.

  V. He Instructed His Team (Matt. 10:5—11:1)

    A. He told <u>them</u> what they had to do (vv. 5-8).

    B. He told them what they should <u>not</u> do (vv. 9-10).

    C. He told them what they could <u>expect</u> (v. 10).

    D. He gave them <u>information</u> that they needed (v. 11).

    E. He told them <u>where</u> they should stay (vv. 11-12).

    F. He told them how to <u>respond</u> (vv. 13-15).

  VI. He Gave Responsibility to His Team (Matt. 21:6).

    A. Jesus was the <u>Master</u> Coach.

    B. Jesus allowed them to practice their <u>principles</u>.

  VII. He Gave Them Authority (Luke 9:1).

    He gave them <u>credentials</u>

        1. To enter the <u>stronghold</u> of the enemy

        2. As <u>ambassadors</u> of the King

VIII. He Periodically Evaluated the Work (Luke 10:17).

    A. Kingdom efforts need <u>quality</u> control.

    B. We must evaluate our <u>influence</u>.

    C. Evaluation reveals necessary <u>adjustments</u>.

IX. He Clearly Articulated the Mission (Matt. 28:19-20).

    A. Go and <u>make</u> disciples.

    B. When the church puts this into practice, it becomes a living organism that <u>reproduces</u> itself.

X. He Enabled the Team (Luke 24:49).

    A. The <u>promise</u> is fulfilled (Luke 24:49).

    B. Before <u>Pentecost</u>.

    C. <u>After</u> Pentecost.

EACH ONE WIN ONE

Intro.: Evangelism Is Not Accidental!
- A. Evangelism happens on <u>purpose</u>.
  - 1. It will take a plan to reach the <u>unchurched</u>.
  - 2. When one person <u>catches</u> the vision.
- B. The <u>Holy Spirit</u> wants to help us build the church.
  - 1. To <u>impact</u> our community
  - 2. To start new <u>churches</u>

I. The Purpose
- A. Each One Win One is based on <u>biblical</u> principles.
- B. Every believer is a part of that <u>plan</u>.

II. Preparing the Church Through Prayer

Every church has its own <u>personality</u>.
  - 1. Not <u>every</u> evangelistic strategy fits.
  - 2. It begins with the <u>pastor</u>.

III. The Dedication Service
- A. The strategy is <u>launched</u>.
- B. The <u>moment</u> of dedication

  Call for <u>commitment</u> to
  - *a.* Try to win <u>one</u> person to Christ
  - *b.* Pray that <u>God</u> will help
  - *c.* List the persons for whom they will be <u>praying</u>.
  - *d.* <u>Disciple</u> the new Christian.

IV. The Follow-up

Intro.: Promotion should take place <u>every</u> week.
- A. <u>Share</u> the results.
- B. Introduce the new <u>converts</u>.
- C. Prepare a <u>certificate</u> of recognition for each one who has won someone to Christ.
- D. Schedule prayer <u>meetings</u>.

V. Drawing the <u>Net</u>: Receiving New Members
- A. Allow the congregation to see the importance of <u>membership</u>.
  - 1. It <u>creates</u> enthusiasm.
  - 2. It creates <u>victory</u>.
  - 3. It <u>motivates</u>.
  - 4. It <u>sets</u> goals.
  - 5. It helps fulfill the <u>Great</u> Commission.
  - 6. It <u>stimulates</u> growth.
- B. Preparing the <u>new</u> converts.
  - 1. Create membership <u>classes</u>.
  - 2. <u>Elements</u> of membership that should be included
    - *a.* <u>Mentors</u> invited to stand with the new convert.
    - *b.* Share how God has <u>blessed</u> each new convert.
    - *c.* Ask for a <u>testimony</u> from each new convert.

      d. Explain the Each One Win One <u>plan</u> and call for new commitments.

      e. Invite the convert to win a <u>new person</u> to Christ.

      f. Invite the mentors to win <u>another</u> person to Christ.

VI. Overcoming Evangelism Barriers

    A. The <u>Devil</u> (1 Pet. 5:8)

    B. <u>Tradition</u>

    C. Disorganization

    D. Insincerity

    E. Fear

    F. <u>Inferiority</u>

THE BIG BROTHERS AND BIG SISTERS MODEL

Intro.: Big Brothers and Big Sisters Model

    A. <u>Adequate</u> follow-up.

    B. <u>Disciple</u> the new believers.

  I. Presentation of the Big Brothers and Big Sisters Model

    A. Begins with a service of <u>dedication</u>

    B. A <u>service</u> of consecration

    C. Basic steps

       1. <u>Praying</u> for 10 unsaved friends

       2. Inviting those 10 to an <u>evangelistic</u> campaign

       3. Discipling those who <u>accept</u> Christ

    D. Holding the consecration <u>service</u> for Big Brothers and Big Sisters

 II. The Big Brothers and Big Sisters Meeting

<u>Selling</u> the plan

       1. Begin with <u>prayer</u>.

       2. Read 2 Tim. 2:2.

       3. Ask each person to <u>pray</u> for 10 people.

       4. <u>Explain</u> what Big Brothers and Big Sisters are to do.

          a. Pray each day for the <u>salvation</u> of every person on their list.

          b. Become accountable <u>daily</u>.

          c. Following the <u>60</u> days, invite all 10 to the evangelistic campaign.

       5. Explain the <u>work</u> of the Big Brothers and Big Sisters.

          a. Identify all who <u>attend</u>.

          b. Encourage those who attend to <u>decide</u> for Christ.

          c. <u>Identify</u> all who accept Christ as their personal Savior.

       6. Explain the work of Big <u>Brothers</u> and Big Sisters after the evangelistic campaign.

          a. Disciple the <u>new believer</u>.

          b. Make a <u>personal</u> visit to every person that you invited.

          c. Begin a <u>discipleship course</u> with the new believer.

          d. Teach new <u>believers</u> the basics.

          e. Talk to the new believers about the <u>infilling</u> of the Holy Spirit.

          f. <u>Invite</u> new believers to the local church.

          g. Guide new believers toward <u>baptism</u>.

          h. Invite new believers to <u>membership</u>.

          i. Ask the <u>new</u> believer to become a Big Brother and Big Sister.

III. Characteristics of Big Brothers and Big Sisters

    A. They <u>pray</u>.

    B. They are <u>members</u> of the local church.

    C. They have taken a basic course in <u>discipleship</u>.

    D. They are <u>faithful</u>.

    E. They are <u>willing</u>.

A11

PRAYER CELLS

I. The Purpose of Prayer Cells
   A. To <u>pray</u> (Acts 4:23-31)
   B. To <u>increase</u> the Kingdom

II. The Biblical <u>Basis</u> for Prayer Cells (Acts 2:46)

III. Strategies for <u>Starting</u> Prayer Cells
   A. How <u>many</u> need to be started?
   B. What types of <u>homes</u>?
   C. <u>Where</u> to meet?

IV. What Happens in the Prayer <u>Cells</u>?
   A. The <u>agenda</u>
   B. The <u>leaders</u>
      One of the leaders <u>records</u>
      1. Prayer <u>requests</u>
      2. Corresponding <u>number</u> for each request
      3. The <u>date</u> of each prayer request
      4. Names and <u>addresses</u>
      5. Dates of <u>answered</u> prayers
      6. The chapter of Acts <u>read</u>

V. What to <u>Avoid</u>
   A. The cells should not include <u>preaching</u> or in-depth study.
   B. Leadership should not come from any church but the <u>mother</u> church.
   C. Food and refreshments should <u>not</u> be served.
   D. The meeting should not last longer than <u>45</u> minutes to an hour.
   E. The three <u>leaders</u> should not belong to any other prayer cell.
   F. Prayer requests should not be focused on <u>believers'</u> needs alone.
   G. The <u>unconverted</u> should not be invited.

VI. <u>Who</u> Is Targeted?
   A. The pastor must encourage <u>every</u> believer in the mother church to join a prayer cell.
   B. The pastor should watch for members of the congregation who are <u>gifted</u> in prayer cell leadership.
   C. <u>Caution</u> should be used in selecting core leadership.
   D. Prayer cell leaders should come from the <u>covenant</u> membership of the church.
   E. The <u>pastor</u> is primary in developing leadership for the prayer cells.

VII. How Is <u>Leadership</u> Expanded?
   A. The <u>role</u> of the pastor
   B. Discovering the <u>commitment</u> of leaders
   C. <u>Multiplying</u> leaders

VIII. The Discipleship Cell (The <u>Mother</u> Cell)
   A. Leaders should be given <u>solid</u> spiritual food through Bible study.

B. Prayer cell <u>strategies</u> should be taught.

C. Leaders should be motivated to carry out the <u>church's</u> mission.

D. <u>Leaders</u> need to ask questions and discuss problems.

E. There should be an <u>evaluation</u> of what is taking place in each of the prayer cells.

IX. <u>Benefits</u> of a Prayer Cell

A. It <u>stimulates</u> the development of workers.

B. The church and the pastor are <u>decentralized</u>.

C. <u>Prayer</u> is systematically offered for specific needs.

D. There is <u>growth</u> in the local church.

EVANGELISTIC CAMPAIGNS

Intro.: Do the Work in Advance

    A. Evangelistic campaigns take <u>perspiration</u>.

    B. Evangelistic campaigns take <u>inspiration</u>.

    C. The principles of evangelism

        1. God does not want any to <u>perish</u>.

        2. God wants <u>everyone</u> to come into the Kingdom.

        3. He <u>acts</u> in accordance to His will.

        4. He wants the believer to be <u>sanctified</u>.

  I. How Evangelistic Campaigns Work

    A. Big Brothers and Big <u>Sisters</u>

        1. Consecrate Big Brothers and Big <u>Sisters</u> two <u>months</u> in advance.

        2. <u>Begin</u> to pray for 10 people.

    B. <u>Prayer</u> cells

        1. Begin prayer cells <u>three</u> months in advance.

        2. Invite <u>unsaved persons</u> who have been prayed for to these campaigns three weeks in advance.

  II. Planning for an Ever-Increasing Harvest

    A. Six months in advance

    Intro.: Begin to <u>implement</u> Big Brothers and Big Sisters and prayer cell plans.

        1. Big Brothers and Big Sisters should begin working with all who <u>accepted</u> Christ in the previous campaign.

        2. <u>Invite</u> new converts to baptism class.

        3. Develop <u>sermon</u> theme based on *Basic Bible Studies* for new converts.

        4. <u>Fellowship</u> should be planned for new converts and the church.

        5. Pastor should begin <u>follow-up</u> in Big Brothers and Big Sisters.

        6. Prayer cells should be <u>evaluated</u>.

        7. A new <u>cycle</u> of prayer cells should be launched.

            a. A <u>local</u> coordinator should be appointed.

            b. Areas of the <u>community</u> should be targeted.

            c. <u>Homes</u> should be chosen.

            d. Leaders should be <u>trained</u>.

    B. Five months in advance

        1. New <u>converts</u> should have completed the membership class.

        2. The Each One Win One <u>plan</u> should be reimplemented.

        3. Big Brothers and Big Sisters should <u>continue</u> their work.

        4. The pastor should continue to <u>promote</u> prayer cells.

        5. Remind the congregation of our call to win the <u>lost</u>.

    C. Four months in advance

        1. New converts should be guided in <u>discovering</u> their spiritual gifts.

        2. Promote Theological <u>Education</u> by Extension.

        3. <u>Preach</u> on the infilling of the Holy Spirit.

        4. Big Brothers and Big Sisters should continue to do their <u>work</u>.

        5. <u>Prayer</u> cells should be evaluated.

D. Three months in advance
   1. Be aware of those who are not attending church <u>regularly</u>.
   2. Set <u>date</u> for Big Brothers and Big Sisters consecration service.
   3. Posters, <u>flyers</u>, and Big Brothers and Big Sisters forms should be printed.
   4. Preach on the need to impact the <u>city</u> for Christ.
   5. Hold a prayer cell <u>evaluation</u>, including which prayer cells should become missions and which missions should become a new church.

E. Two months in advance
   1. Big Brothers and Big Sisters should be <u>consecrated</u>.
   2. The Each One Win One <u>poster</u> should continue to be displayed.
   3. <u>Train</u> Big Brothers and Big Sisters.
   4. Seek to <u>involve</u> as many people as possible.
   5. Promote plans <u>weekly</u>.
   6. The evangelistic campaign should be <u>promoted</u>.
   7. Prayer cell <u>celebration</u> services should be scheduled.

F. One month in advance
   1. <u>Altar</u> workers should be trained.
   2. <u>Neighborhoods</u> should be canvassed.
   3. Celebration services should be <u>conducted</u>.
   4. Big Brothers and Big Sisters should be reminded to <u>invite</u> the 10 they have been praying for.
   5. The <u>multiplication</u> of prayer cells should be planned.

G. Conduct the evangelistic campaign.

III. Results of an Evangelistic Campaign
   A. <u>Accelerated</u> church multiplication will result.
   B. <u>Churches</u> will be established.

IV. Citywide Evangelistic Campaigns
   A. Produced under a spirit of <u>cooperation</u>.
   B. Evangelistic <u>campaigns</u> still work if they are worked.

MULTIPLYING CHURCHES AND PASTORS

Intro.: A Mind-set That Contributes to Growth (Acts 2:44-45)

    A. The <u>Early</u> Church was concerned with mission.

    B. The result was accelerated <u>growth</u>.

  I. Each Church Plant a Church

    A. The <u>mission</u>

       1. Prayer cells <u>grow</u> into a mission.

       2. The mission is <u>established</u>.

    B. The <u>new</u> church

       1. The mission grows by establishing its own <u>prayer</u> cells.

       2. New <u>people</u> are invited to become part of the mission.

       3. The mission is given the opportunity to become its own <u>church</u>.

       4. The new church is <u>organized</u>.

       5. The new church continues to <u>grow</u>.

 II. New Church Pastors

    A. The "growing church" <u>problem</u>

       1. Resources.

       2. How will the new <u>pastor</u> fit into the new church?

       3. <u>Fewer</u> young people entering ministry.

    B. The new <u>solution</u>

       1. Laypersons are <u>potential</u> pastors.

       2. Its roots are in the Early <u>Church</u>.

       3. <u>How</u> is this accomplished?

          a. Each pastor <u>trains</u> leaders in the discipleship cell.

          b. Potential pastors will be given the opportunity to <u>lead</u> missions.

       4. Trusting <u>God</u> to supply.

III. Support Systems

    A. Education by <u>Extension</u>

    B. Involving the <u>educational</u> institutions

    C. <u>Opportunities</u> for educational institutions

    D. Added <u>benefits</u> of Education by Extension

IMPACT: COORDINATING THE PLANS

Intro.: IMPACT:

<u>I</u>nvolving <u>M</u>embers, <u>P</u>astors, <u>A</u>nd <u>C</u>hurches in <u>T</u>andem

I. IMPACT Leadership
   A. <u>Humility</u> (1 Pet. 5:5)
   B. <u>Faithfulness</u> (1 Cor. 4:2)
   C. <u>Hardworking</u>

II. The IMPACT Plan
   <u>Four</u> stages
   A. Preparation
   B. <u>Expansion</u>
   C. Consolidation
   D. <u>Multiplication</u>

III. Steps That Will IMPACT Your City
   A. Preparation
      1. <u>Internal</u> preparation
         a. Preparing the <u>mind</u>
         b. <u>Casting</u> the vision
         c. Focusing <u>ministry</u>
         d. Intensifying <u>effort</u>
         e. <u>Preparing</u> the team
         f. Preparing the <u>church</u>
      2. <u>External</u> preparation
         a. The local church must become acquainted with the <u>city</u>.
         b. The <u>local</u> church must familiarize itself with its own area.
         c. Develop the <u>battle</u> plan.
      3. <u>Strategic</u> preparation
         a. Plan what <u>methods</u> you will employ.
         b. <u>Understand</u> philosophies and terminologies of the various plans.
         c. A system of growth must be <u>planned</u>.
         d. <u>Trained</u> IMPACT coordinators:
            (1) District coordinators with <u>district</u> leadership.
            (2) Local coordinators are selected by the <u>pastor</u> to help assist.
      4. <u>Spiritual</u> preparation
         a. Take the city in the <u>name</u> of the Lord.
         b. Claim the <u>promise</u> of God.
         c. Prepare for <u>opposition</u>.
         d. First stage of preparation:
            (1) Set <u>strategy</u>.
            (2) Emphasis on <u>spiritual</u> growth.
   B. Expansion
      1. Set a <u>retreat</u>.
         a. <u>Inform</u> and inspire pastors.
         b. <u>Evaluate</u> the present position.

     c. A possible change in <u>direction</u>.

     d. Are we <u>willing</u> to take on this task?

     e. A <u>ministry</u> strategy is determined.

     f. A <u>faith</u> goal is established.

     g. Introduce <u>team</u>.

  2. Evaluate the prayer <u>cells</u> (second quarter).

     a. Evaluate the cells in the <u>local</u> church.
<u>Meet</u> with district leadership.

       (1) Have a <u>review</u> of how prayer cells function.

       (2) Display the map of cells and missions that have <u>opened</u>.

       (3) Leadership should be <u>introduced</u>.

       (4) Include a review of <u>answered</u> prayers.

       (5) Provide a time for <u>testimonies</u>.

     b. Conduct a <u>seminar</u> on IMPACT.

     c. Have a celebration <u>service</u>.

  3. <u>Consecration</u> of Big Brothers/Big Sisters.

     a. <u>Materials</u> will be distributed.

     b. Instruction will be <u>given</u>.

     c. Talk about successes for <u>encouragement</u>.

  4. Evangelistic <u>campaigns</u>.

     a. Held on three levels.

       (1) Celebration <u>service</u>

       (2) Local <u>church</u> evangelistic campaigns held

       (3) <u>City</u>wide campaign follows up local campaign

     b. Give special <u>recognition</u>.

     c. Make an <u>announcement</u> of future plans.

C. Consolidation

  1. <u>New</u> churches organized.

  2. Evangelism and discipleship efforts will be <u>expanded</u>; share past <u>experiences</u>.

D. Multiplication

  1. The miracle of <u>multiplication</u>.

  2. <u>IMPACT</u> produces results!

GOALS AND LEADERSHIP

Intro.: Early Church Leadership

    A. Paul had a <u>passion</u> for Christ (Phil. 3:7-11).

    B. Paul was passionate about <u>winning</u> souls (1 Cor. 9:16-22).

    C. Paul was <u>passionate</u> about doing things the right way (Titus 3:14).

    D. Paul was passionate about setting a course of <u>action</u> for his life (Phil. 3:12-16).

  I. Vision

    A. Setting goals for the vision
       Guidelines

      1. Goals should be <u>written</u> out.

      2. Goals should be <u>promoted</u>.

      3. Goals should be definite and <u>measurable</u>.

      4. Goals should be <u>evaluated</u>.

      5. Goals should be set in <u>faith</u>.

      6. Goals should be <u>guided</u> by the Holy Spirit.

    B. Reaching goals

      1. Goals should be <u>reachable</u>.

      2. Goals should have <u>long</u>-range and short-range dimensions.

      3. Goal <u>barriers</u> should be dealt with.

      4. <u>Motivation</u> should be used to reach goals.
         What motivates <u>Christians</u> to reach goals?

         a. <u>Biblical</u> preaching

         b. <u>Promotion</u>

         c. <u>Incentives</u>

         d. <u>Recognition</u>

         e. Example

  II. The Leader and the Team

    A. <u>Form</u> the team.

    B. <u>Supervise</u> the team.

    C. <u>Motivate</u> the team.

      1. Enthusiasm.

      2. <u>Relationship</u>.

      3. Reporting.

      4. <u>Encouraging</u>.

      5. Freedom.

  III. Where Do We Go from Here?

    A. We've <u>examined</u> the plans.

    B. We've cast the <u>vision</u>.

    C. We've set some <u>reachable</u> goals.

    D. Now what?

      1. We <u>pray</u>.

      2. We <u>practice</u>.

      3. We <u>plan</u>.

      4. We <u>project</u>.

APPENDIX B
STUDENT OUTLINES

THE SOUTH AMERICAN STRATEGY

I. A New Mentality

    A. Developing spiritual communities

        1. Spiritual commitment resulted in numerical _____ (Acts 16:5).

        2. Be willing to use a new _____ to reach as many as possible (1 Cor. 9:12-23).

    B. Back to the New Testament

        1. Employ _____ methods.

        2. Move from exclusive to _____ (Acts 10:34).

II. A Plan of Mobilization: Each One Win One

    A. Total _____ becomes a priority.

    B. The challenge to win _____.

III. The Power of Our Witness

    A. Growth begins with _____ believers.

        1. _____ relationships influence the lost.

        2. The gospel _____ begins by reaching one person.

    B. The key to evangelism is not programming but _____.

        1. Many _____ have a desire for someone to love them.

        2. What happens when the whole _____ expresses love and interest?

IV. An Emphasis on Natural Growth

    A. The natural growth of the _____.

        1. It must have a heart that is _____ in ministry (2 Cor. 8:1-5).

        2. The church doesn't grow because of its _____; rather it grows because of its Source (Zech. 4:6).

    B. _____ church multiplication does not depend on outside resources.

        1. We must have a deep concern for the _____.

        2. We must be willing to give of our _____ resources.

V. The Infilling of the Holy Spirit

    A. The _____ call

        1. Every believer must be _____ with the Holy Spirit.

        2. The power to _____.

    B. _____ this message

        1. With _____!

        2. With _____!

VI. A Spirit of Giving

    Raising the level of _____

        1. There must be a commitment to _____ the kingdom of God.

        2. Aggressive church multiplication begins with a spirit of _____.

VII. The Power of the Team

    A. Team _____ includes

        1. A _____ to share

        2. Joining _____

    B. Developing an evangelistic _____

        1. _____ churches

        2. Citywide _____

VIII. Empowering the Laity

    A. Total _____ of the laity

        1. Guidance through _____

        2. _____-inspired initiatives

    B. The expectation to _____ new churches

        1. Go and make _____.

        2. Rapid _____ demands the laity to be mobilized.

  IX. The Call to Take Up the Cross

    The emphasis on _____

        1. _____ suffering (Acts 5:17-42)

        2. Dedicated _____

   X. Decentralizing Theological Education

    Education by _____

        1. Taking the _____ to the people

        2. A _____ resource of trained pastors

A BIBLICAL AND HISTORICAL STRATEGY

Intro.: Accelerated Church Multiplication

    A. How the Holy Spirit worked in _____
        1. The Church _____ (Acts 4:4).
        2. The Church _____ (Acts 6:7).
        3. The Church _____ (Acts 9:31).
        4. The Church's _____ was far-reaching (Acts 11:21).
        5. The Church was _____ (Acts 12:24).
    B. Paul's _____
        1. To point people to _____
        2. To _____ new believers
        3. To _____ for leadership

  I. Strategies That Impact the World

    A. Aggressive _____ multiplication
        1. Catching the _____
        2. _____ our world
    B. The _____
        1. Impact _____
        2. Impact _____
        3. Impact _____
        4. Impact _____
        5. Impact _____ and countries

 II. By the Book

    Intro.: Our strategy is _____ on the Word of God
        1. The _____ of the Holy Spirit's power (Acts 1:8)
        2. The promise of the Holy Spirit's _____ (John 16:13)
    A. The Example of Moses (Exod. 18)
        1. The _____ account
        2. The _____
    B. The Need for External Leadership
        1. Taking the message to the _____
        2. _____ and make disciples (Matt. 28:19)
    C. The Example of Paul
        1. Paul's aim was not only to grow churches but also to grow _____.
        2. His _____—to exalt Christ.
        3. His _____—to mentor others.
        4. His method—to _____ additional leaders.
    D. The Best Leader of All—Jesus
        1. Jesus' leadership _____ alone.
            a. He _____ the world.
            b. He employed external _____.
            c. His _____ was successful.
        2. Jesus still calls His Church to follow Him.
           Operating at _____ important levels
            a. Level One—_____

       b. Level Two—_____
       c. Level Three—_____ churches
       d. Level Four—_____ churches

III. Overcoming Church Problems
   A. It overcomes by _____.
   B. It overcomes by _____.
   C. It overcomes by _____.

IV. The Potential
   A. Believers have incredible _____.
   B. Believers can _____ their world.

V. Follow the Leaders
   A. It's up to _____!
   B. Be a part of a movement that _____ your world.

THE JESUS STRATEGY

Intro.: The Life and Ministry of Jesus
    A. It changed _____.
    B. It changed _____.

  I. Jesus Depended on His Father (John 12:49).
    A. He depended on His Father for His _____ and ministry.
    B. Jesus began and ended His ministry by _____ to His Father (Matt. 4; Luke 22:42).
    C. Jesus prayed for His _____ (John 17:1-21).
        1. He _____ His ministry purpose.
        2. He communicated His _____.
        3. He _____ His disciples.
        4. He _____ His strategy.

  II. Jesus Had an Evangelistic Purpose (Luke 19:10).
    A. He was _____ on the main thing.
    B. He was _____ sidetracked.
    C. He coordinated His _____.

  III. Jesus Wisely Selected His Disciples (Matt. 10).
    A. He found workers and put them to _____ work.
    B. He _____ chose His disciples.

  IV. He Motivated His Disciples (Luke 10:22-24).
    A. After selecting His disciples, He _____ them.
    B. He spent _____ with His disciples.
    C. He took great _____ in His disciples.

  V. He Instructed His Team (Matt. 10:5—11:1)
    A. He told _____ what they had to do (vv. 5-8).
    B. He told them what they should _____ do (vv. 9-10).
    C. He told them what they could _____ (v. 10).
    D. He gave them _____ that they needed (v. 11).
    E. He told them _____ they should stay (vv. 11-12).
    F. He told them how to _____ (vv. 13-15).

  VI. He Gave Responsibility to His Team (Matt. 21:6).
    A. Jesus was the _____ Coach.
    B. Jesus allowed them to practice their _____.

  VII. He Gave Them Authority (Luke 9:1).
    He gave them _____
        1. To enter the _____ of the enemy
        2. As _____ of the King

  VIII. He Periodically Evaluated the Work (Luke 10:17).
    A. Kingdom efforts need _____ control.
    B. We must evaluate our _____.

C. Evaluation reveals necessary _____.

IX. He Clearly Articulated the Mission (Matt. 28:19-20).

  A. Go and _____ disciples.

  B. When the church puts this into practice, it becomes a living organism that _____ itself.

X. He Enabled the Team (Luke 24:49).

  A. The _____ is fulfilled (Luke 24:49).

  B. Before _____.

  C. _____ Pentecost.

EACH ONE WIN ONE

Intro.: Evangelism Is Not Accidental!

    A. Evangelism happens on _____.

        1. It will take a plan to reach the _____.

        2. When one person _____ the vision.

    B. The _____ wants to help us build the church.

        1. To _____ our community

        2. To start new _____

  I. The Purpose

    A. Each One Win One is based on _____ principles.

    B. Every believer is a part of that _____.

 II. Preparing the Church Through Prayer

    Every church has its own _____.

        1. Not _____ evangelistic strategy fits.

        2. It begins with the _____.

III. The Dedication Service

    A. The strategy is _____.

    B. The _____ of dedication

    Call for _____ to

        a. Try to win _____ person to Christ

        b. Pray that _____ will help

        c. List the persons for whom they will be _____.

        d. _____ the new Christian.

IV. The Follow-up

    Intro.: Promotion should take place _____ week.

    A. _____ the results.

    B. Introduce the new _____.

    C. Prepare a _____ of recognition for each one who has won someone to Christ.

    D. Schedule prayer _____.

  V. Drawing the _____: Receiving New Members

    A. Allow the congregation to see the importance of _____.

        1. It _____ enthusiasm.

        2. It creates _____.

        3. It _____.

        4. It _____ goals.

        5. It helps fulfill the _____ Commission.

        6. It _____ growth.

    B. Preparing the _____ converts.

        1. Create membership _____.

        2. _____ of membership that should be included

            a. _____ invited to stand with the new convert.

            b. Share how God has _____ each new convert.

            c. Ask for a _____ from each new convert.

      d. Explain the Each One Win One _____ and call for new commitments.

      e. Invite the convert to win a _____ to Christ.

      f. Invite the mentors to win _____ person to Christ.

VI. Overcoming Evangelism Barriers

    A. The _____ (1 Pet. 5:8)

    B. _____

    C. Disorganization

    D. Insincerity

    E. Fear

    F. _____

THE BIG BROTHERS AND BIG SISTERS MODEL

Intro.: Big Brothers and Big Sisters Model

   A. _____ follow-up.

   B. _____ the new believers.

  I. Presentation of the Big Brothers and Big Sisters Model

   A. Begins with a service of _____

   B. A _____ of consecration

   C. Basic steps

     1. _____ for 10 unsaved friends

     2. Inviting those 10 to an _____ campaign

     3. Discipling those who _____ Christ

   D. Holding the consecration _____ for Big Brothers and Big Sisters

 II. The Big Brothers and Big Sisters Meeting

   _____ the plan

     1. Begin with _____.

     2. Read 2 Tim. 2:2.

     3. Ask each person to _____ for 10 people.

     4. _____ what Big Brothers and Big Sisters are to do.

       a. Pray each day for the _____ of every person on their list.

       b. Become accountable _____.

       c. Following the _____ days, invite all 10 to the evangelistic campaign.

     5. Explain the _____ of the Big Brothers and Big Sisters.

       a. Identify all who _____.

       b. Encourage those who attend to _____ for Christ.

       c. _____ all who accept Christ as their personal Savior.

     6. Explain the work of Big _____ and Big Sisters after the evangelistic campaign.

       a. Disciple the _____.

       b. Make a _____ visit to every person that you invited.

       c. Begin a _____ with the new believer.

       d. Teach new _____ the basics.

       e. Talk to the new believers about the _____ of the Holy Spirit.

       f. _____ new believers to the local church.

       g. Guide new believers toward _____.

       h. Invite new believers to _____.

       i. Ask the _____ believer to become a Big Brother and Big Sister.

III. Characteristics of Big Brothers and Big Sisters

   A. They _____.

   B. They are _____ of the local church.

   C. They have taken a basic course in _____.

   D. They are _____.

   E. They are _____.

PRAYER CELLS

I. The Purpose of Prayer Cells
    A. To _____ (Acts 4:23-31)
    B. To _____ the Kingdom

II. The Biblical _____ for Prayer Cells (Acts 2:46)

III. Strategies for _____ Prayer Cells
    A. How _____ need to be started?
    B. What types of _____?
    C. _____ to meet?

IV. What Happens in the Prayer _____?
    A. The _____
    B. The _____
    One of the leaders _____
    1. Prayer _____
    2. Corresponding _____ for each request
    3. The _____ of each prayer request
    4. Names and _____
    5. Dates of _____ prayers
    6. The chapter of Acts _____

V. What to _____
    A. The cells should not include _____ or in-depth study.
    B. Leadership should not come from any church but the _____ church.
    C. Food and refreshments should _____ be served.
    D. The meeting should not last longer than _____ minutes to an hour.
    E. The three _____ should not belong to any other prayer cell.
    F. Prayer requests should not be focused on _____ needs alone.
    G. The _____ should not be invited.

VI. _____ Is Targeted?
    A. The pastor must encourage _____ believer in the mother church to join a prayer cell.
    B. The pastor should watch for members of the congregation who are _____ in prayer cell leadership.
    C. _____ should be used in selecting core leadership.
    D. Prayer cell leaders should come from the _____ membership of the church.
    E. The _____ is primary in developing leadership for the prayer cells.

VII. How Is _____ Expanded?
    A. The _____ of the pastor
    B. Discovering the _____ of leaders
    C. _____ leaders

VIII. The Discipleship Cell (The _____ Cell)
    A. Leaders should be given _____ spiritual food through Bible study.

B. Prayer cell _____ should be taught.

C. Leaders should be motivated to carry out the _____ mission.

D. _____ need to ask questions and discuss problems.

E. There should be an _____ of what is taking place in each of the prayer cells.

IX. _____ of a Prayer Cell

A. It _____ the development of workers.

B. The church and the pastor are _____.

C. _____ is systematically offered for specific needs.

D. There is _____ in the local church.

EVANGELISTIC CAMPAIGNS

Intro.: Do the Work in Advance

    A. Evangelistic campaigns take _____.

    B. Evangelistic campaigns take _____.

    C. The principles of evangelism

        1. God does not want any to _____.

        2. God wants _____ to come into the Kingdom.

        3. He _____ in accordance to His will.

        4. He wants the believer to be _____.

  I. How Evangelistic Campaigns Work

    A. Big Brothers and Big _____

        1. Consecrate Big Brothers and Big _____ two _____ in advance.

        2. _____ to pray for 10 people.

    B. _____ cells

        1. Begin prayer cells _____ months in advance.

        2. Invite _____ who have been prayed for to these campaigns three weeks in advance.

 II. Planning for an Ever-Increasing Harvest

    A. Six months in advance

       Intro.: Begin to _____ Big Brothers and Big Sisters and prayer cell plans.

        1. Big Brothers and Big Sisters should begin working with all who _____ Christ in the previous campaign.

        2. _____ new converts to baptism class.

        3. Develop _____ theme based on *Basic Bible Studies* for new converts.

        4. _____ should be planned for new converts and the church.

        5. Pastor should begin _____ in Big Brothers and Big Sisters.

        6. Prayer cells should be _____.

        7. A new _____ of prayer cells should be launched.

          a. A _____ coordinator should be appointed.

          b. Areas of the _____ should be targeted.

          c. _____ should be chosen.

          d. Leaders should be _____.

    B. Five months in advance

        1. New _____ should have completed the membership class.

        2. The Each One Win One _____ should be reimplemented.

        3. Big Brothers and Big Sisters should _____ their work.

        4. The pastor should continue to _____ prayer cells.

        5. Remind the congregation of our call to win the _____.

    C. Four months in advance

        1. New converts should be guided in _____ their spiritual gifts.

        2. Promote Theological _____ by Extension.

        3. _____ on the infilling of the Holy Spirit.

        4. Big Brothers and Big Sisters should continue to do their _____.

        5. _____ cells should be evaluated.

D. Three months in advance
1. Be aware of those who are not attending church _____.
2. Set _____ for Big Brothers and Big Sisters consecration service.
3. Posters, _____, and Big Brothers and Big Sisters forms should be printed.
4. Preach on the need to impact the _____ for Christ.
5. Hold a prayer cell _____, including which prayer cells should become missions and which missions should become a new church.

E. Two months in advance
1. Big Brothers and Big Sisters should be _____.
2. The Each One Win One _____ should continue to be displayed.
3. _____ Big Brothers and Big Sisters.
4. Seek to _____ as many people as possible.
5. Promote plans _____.
6. The evangelistic campaign should be _____.
7. Prayer cell _____ services should be scheduled.

F. One month in advance
1. _____ workers should be trained.
2. _____ should be canvassed.
3. Celebration services should be _____.
4. Big Brothers and Big Sisters should be reminded to _____ the 10 they have been praying for.
5. The _____ of prayer cells should be planned.

G. Conduct the evangelistic campaign.

III. Results of an Evangelistic Campaign
A. _____ church multiplication will result.
B. _____ will be established.

IV. Citywide Evangelistic Campaigns
A. Produced under a spirit of _____.
B. Evangelistic _____ still work if they are worked.

MULTIPLYING CHURCHES AND PASTORS

Intro.: A Mind-set That Contributes to Growth (Acts 2:44-45)

    A. The _____ Church was concerned with mission.

    B. The result was accelerated _____.

  I. Each Church Plant a Church

    A. The _____

       1. Prayer cells _____ into a mission.

       2. The mission is _____.

    B. The _____ church

       1. The mission grows by establishing its own _____ cells.

       2. New _____ are invited to become part of the mission.

       3. The mission is given the opportunity to become its own _____.

       4. The new church is _____.

       5. The new church continues to _____.

  II. New Church Pastors

    A. The "growing church" _____

       1. Resources.

       2. How will the new _____ fit into the new church?

       3. _____ young people entering ministry.

    B. The new _____

       1. Laypersons are _____ pastors.

       2. Its roots are in the Early _____.

       3. _____ is this accomplished?

         a. Each pastor _____ leaders in the discipleship cell.

         b. Potential pastors will be given the opportunity to _____ missions.

       4. Trusting _____ to supply.

 III. Support Systems

    A. Education by _____

    B. Involving the _____ institutions

    C. _____ for educational institutions

    D. Added _____ of Education by Extension

IMPACT: COORDINATING THE PLANS

Intro.: IMPACT:

<u>I</u>nvolving <u>M</u>embers, <u>P</u>astors, <u>A</u>nd <u>C</u>hurches in <u>T</u>andem

I. IMPACT Leadership

  A. _____ (1 Pet. 5:5)

  B. _____ (1 Cor. 4:2)

  C. _____

II. The IMPACT Plan

  _____ stages

  A. Preparation

  B. _____

  C. Consolidation

  D. _____

III. Steps That Will IMPACT Your City

  A. Preparation

    1. _____ preparation

      a. Preparing the _____

      b. _____ the vision

      c. Focusing _____

      d. Intensifying _____

      e. _____ the team

      f. Preparing the _____

    2. _____ preparation

      a. The local church must become acquainted with the _____.

      b. The _____ church must familiarize itself with its own area.

      c. Develop the _____ plan.

    3. _____ preparation

      a. Plan what _____ you will employ.

      b. _____ philosophies and terminologies of the various plans.

      c. A system of growth must be _____.

      d. _____ IMPACT coordinators:

        (1) District coordinators with _____ leadership.

        (2) Local coordinators are selected by the _____ to help assist.

    4. _____ preparation

      a. Take the city in the _____ of the Lord.

      b. Claim the _____ of God.

      c. Prepare for _____.

      d. First stage of preparation:

        (1) Set _____.

        (2) Emphasis on _____ growth.

  B. Expansion

    1. Set a _____.

      a. _____ and inspire pastors.

      b. _____ the present position.

  c. A possible change in _____.

  d. Are we _____ to take on this task?

  e. A _____ strategy is determined.

  f. A _____ goal is established.

  g. Introduce _____.

 2. Evaluate the prayer _____ (second quarter).

  a. Evaluate the cells in the _____ church.

  _____ with district leadership.

   (1) Have a _____ of how prayer cells function.

   (2) Display the map of cells and missions that have _____.

   (3) Leadership should be _____.

   (4) Include a review of _____ prayers.

   (5) Provide a time for _____.

  b. Conduct a _____ on IMPACT.

  c. Have a celebration _____.

 3. _____ of Big Brothers/Big Sisters.

  a. _____ will be distributed.

  b. Instruction will be _____.

  c. Talk about successes for _____.

 4. Evangelistic _____.

  a. Held on three levels.

   (1) Celebration _____

   (2) Local _____ evangelistic campaigns held

   (3) _____wide campaign follows up local campaign

  b. Give special _____.

  c. Make an _____ of future plans.

C. Consolidation

 1. _____ churches organized.

 2. Evangelism and discipleship efforts will be _____; share past _____.

D. Multiplication

 1. The miracle of _____.

 2. _____ produces results!

GOALS AND LEADERSHIP

Intro.: Early Church Leadership

    A. Paul had a _____ for Christ (Phil. 3:7-11).

    B. Paul was passionate about _____ souls (1 Cor. 9:16-22).

    C. Paul was _____ about doing things the right way (Titus 3:14).

    D. Paul was passionate about setting a course of _____ for his life (Phil. 3:12-16).

I. Vision

    A. Setting goals for the vision
       Guidelines
       1. Goals should be _____ out.
       2. Goals should be _____.
       3. Goals should be definite and _____.
       4. Goals should be _____.
       5. Goals should be set in _____.
       6. Goals should be _____ by the Holy Spirit.

    B. Reaching goals
       1. Goals should be _____.
       2. Goals should have _____-range and short-range dimensions.
       3. Goal _____ should be dealt with.
       4. _____ should be used to reach goals.
         What motivates _____ to reach goals?
          a. _____ preaching
          b. _____
          c. _____
          d. _____
          e. Example

II. The Leader and the Team

    A. _____ the team.

    B. _____ the team.

    C. _____ the team.
       1. Enthusiasm.
       2. _____.
       3. Reporting.
       4. _____.
       5. Freedom.

III. Where Do We Go from Here?

    A. We've _____ the plans.

    B. We've cast the _____.

    C. We've set some _____ goals.

    D. Now what?
       1. We _____.
       2. We _____.
       3. We _____.
       4. We _____.

APPENDIX C

EACH ONE WIN ONE CHECKLIST

☐ Begin to prepare a series of messages concerning the value of lost souls. (A list of passages on soul winning is found in chapter 4.)

☐ Prepare worship folder inserts, newsletter articles, posters, drama, and PowerPoint presentations. (If you have access to video production, use this medium as well.)

☐ Begin planning and developing strategy, target group, leadership for service of dedication.

☐ Each One Win One is launched with a service of dedication.

☐ Preparation of messages with emphasis on soul winning.

☐ Have posters ready for Each One Win One to be displayed at this service.

☐ Challenge every member of the congregation to
1. Win one person to Christ during the year.
2. Pray that God will help them win one person.
3. List persons whom they will be praying for.
4. Disciple the new Christians.
5. Prepare them for baptism.
6. Encourage them to become members of the church.
7. Stand with them when they are baptized and are received into membership.
8. Train them to become soul winners.

APPENDIX D

FOLLOW-UP CHECKLIST

☐ Follow up weekly.

☐ Show updates weekly on how the church is doing.

☐ Introduce new converts to the congregation.

☐ Prepare a certificate recognizing the people who have won someone to Christ. (A sample certificate is included in Appendix M.)

☐ Schedule prayer meetings weekly.

☐ Receive new members into the church regularly.
The Benefits of Receiving New Members
  ○ It creates enthusiasm.
  ○ It creates victory.
  ○ It motivates.
  ○ It creates goals.
  ○ It fulfills the Great Commission.
  ○ It stimulates growth.

☐ Prepare your new converts for membership.

☐ Invite new converts to come forward with the person who won them to the Lord. (Present certificate to both at this time.)

☐ Share how God has blessed each convert.

☐ Prepare them to give a testimony.

☐ Explain once again the plan of Each One Win One.

APPENDIX E

BIG BROTHERS AND BIG SISTERS CHECKLIST

- [ ] Begin with a service of dedication.
- [ ] Explain the purpose of Big Brothers/Big Sisters.
- [ ] Prepare an informative and enthusiastic message.
- [ ] Remind the congregation of the three basic steps of Big Brothers/Big Sisters.
  - ○ Pray for at least 10 unsaved friends over a two-month period.
  - ○ Invite those they have prayed for to an evangelistic campaign.
  - ○ Disciple those who accept Christ.
- [ ] Big Brothers/Big Sisters sermon outline is included in chapter 5.
- [ ] Plan a Big Brothers/Big Sisters meeting right after the dedication service.
- [ ] Clearly articulate what is involved in being a Big Brother/Big Sister.
  - ○ Begin with prayer.
  - ○ Read 2 Tim. 2:2.
  - ○ Ask each person to think of and list 10 people for whom he or she will be praying.
- [ ] What do Big Brothers/Big Sisters do?
  - ○ Pray for the salvation of the persons listed—each day, by name.
  - ○ Mark an X by a name when you have fulfilled your commitment.
  - ○ Visit each person after two months and invite him or her to the evangelistic campaign.
- [ ] During the campaign
  - ○ Put an X in the corresponding column if a person attends the campaign.
  - ○ Encourage each one to ask Christ into his or her heart during campaign.
  - ○ Put an X in the corresponding column if the person accepts Christ as Savior.
- [ ] After the campaign
  - ○ Begin to disciple the new converts.
  - ○ Visit all on your list, whether or not they accepted Christ.
  - ○ Teach new converts the basics of the Christian life.
  - ○ Show new converts the need for the infilling of the Holy Spirit.
  - ○ Guide new believers toward baptism.
  - ○ Invite new believers to membership.
  - ○ Ask new believers to become Big Brothers/Big Sisters.

APPENDIX F

INSIGHTS INTO SPIRITUAL GIFTS

To whom and how are spiritual gifts given?

1. Every believer is spiritually gifted (1 Pet. 4:10; 1 Cor. 12:7; Eph. 4:7-8).
2. When he or she becomes a Christian (1 Cor. 12:13)
3. With the gift(s) that God chooses for him or her (1 Cor. 12:11, 18)

Note: No one Christian has all the gifts nor is any one gift common to all Christians (1 Cor. 12:12-18).

What is the purpose of spiritual gifts?

1. The glory of God and His Church (1 Pet. 4:10-11)
2. The building up of the Body of Christ (Eph. 4:12)
3. The unity of the Body (Eph. 4:13)
4. The maturity of the Body (Eph. 4:14-15)
5. The growth of the Body (Eph. 4:16)
6. The common good of the Body (Eph. 4:16)

What are the differences between *human talents* and *spiritual gifts*?

Talents	*Gifts*
1. Inherited from forefathers	1. Given by the Holy Spirit
2. Present from natural birth	2. Present from new birth
3. God-given to all members of the human race	3. God-given to members of Christ's Body
4. For human activities	4. For ministry of the Body
5. Can be operated independent of the Holy Spirit	5. Dependent on the Holy Spirit
6. Ministers primarily on a natural level	6. Ministers on a spiritual level
7. Effects are usually temporal/finite	7. Effects are eternal/infinite
8. Glorifies self	8. Glorifies God

What are the differences between the fruit of the Spirit and the gifts of the Spirit?

Fruit	*Gifts*
1. Defines what a Christian is	1. Determines what a Christian does
2. Same in every Christian	2. Different in each Christian
3. Singular	3. Plural
4. Satan cannot imitate	4. Satan can imitate
5. Deals with character	5. Deals with service ministry
6. End in itself	6. Means to an end
7. Permanent/Eternal	7. Will cease
8. According to spirituality and maturity	8. Not according to spirituality

APPENDIX G

PRAYER CELL CHECKLIST

☐ Become familiar with the purpose of prayer cells (chapter 5).

☐ Remember that the desired end to prayer cells is to start new missions and churches.

☐ Become familiar with the biblical basis of prayer cells (chapter 5).

☐ Determine the strategy for prayer cells.
  ○ How many should we have?
  ○ What types of homes?
  ○ Strategize where they should meet!
  ○ Become familiar with what happens in prayer cells.
    • The agenda
    • The leaders

☐ Remember each leader is to train two other leaders.

☐ Write down the following information.
  ○ Prayer requests
  ○ A corresponding number for each request
  ○ The date of the prayer request
  ○ Names and address and other observations of the unsaved

APPENDIX H

THE EVANGELISTIC CAMPAIGN CHECKLIST

☐ Become familiar with how evangelistic campaigns work.

☐ Three months in advance, begin your prayer cells.

☐ Two months prior to campaign, participants in the Big Brothers/Big Sisters plan are consecrated.

After campaign has ended

☐ Have an afternoon fellowship for all new converts and church members.

☐ Big Brothers/Big Sisters need to begin working with those who have accepted Christ.

☐ Invite all converts to baptism.

☐ Prepare a Sunday night sermon series or pastor's welcome class or video presentation or midweek Bible study on basic Bible study principles.

☐ Pastor begins follow-up meetings with Big Brothers/Big Sisters.

☐ Prayer cells that have been operating for the past three months should be evaluated. Should they become missions? Should they become new church plants?

☐ A new cycle of prayer cells should be launched. (See chapter 6.)

Five months in advance of next campaign

☐ New converts from last campaign should have completed membership class.

☐ Each One Win One should begin again, calling for new people to become involved.

☐ Big Brothers/Big Sisters should continue their work with new converts.

☐ The pastor should continue to promote prayer cells.

☐ The pastor should regularly remind congregation of the need to win people to Christ.

Four months in advance

☐ New members should be guided into spiritual gifts discovery. (See Appendixes F and Q10-Q11 for additional resources.)

☐ The pastor should promote Theological Education by Extension. (See your district leader for information.)

☐ The pastor should preach on the infilling of the Holy Spirit.

☐ Big Brothers/Big Sisters should continue to work with new converts.

☐ Prayer cells should continue to be evaluated.

Three months in advance

☐ Be aware of those who are not attending on a regular basis or those who have dropped out.

☐ Set new dates for Big Brothers/Big Sisters consecration service.

☐ Develop posters and flyers concerning Big Brothers/Big Sisters program.

☐ Preach on the need to impact your community and city.

☐ Evaluate prayer cells.

Two months in advance

☐ New Big Brothers/Big Sisters should be consecrated. (See chapter 5.)

☐ Each One Win One posters should be displayed.

☐ The pastor and assistants should train Big Brothers/Big Sisters.

☐ Seek to involve as many people as possible.

☐ Promote Big Brothers/Big Sisters plan weekly.

☐ Promote the evangelistic campaign.

☐ Prayer cells celebration service should be scheduled. (See chapter 7.)

One month in advance

☐ Altar workers should be trained.

☐ Neighborhoods around the church should be canvassed.

☐ Celebration service for prayer cells should be held.

☐ Big Brothers/Big Sisters should be asked to invite their top 10.

☐ The multiplication of prayer cells should be planned and determine who leaders should be.

Conduct the evangelistic campaign.

Repeat the cycle!

APPENDIX I

MY TOP 10
COMMITMENT LIST

Name	Prayed	Invited	Attended	Accepted
_____	_____	_____	_____	_____
_____	_____	_____	_____	_____
_____	_____	_____	_____	_____
_____	_____	_____	_____	_____
_____	_____	_____	_____	_____
_____	_____	_____	_____	_____
_____	_____	_____	_____	_____
_____	_____	_____	_____	_____
_____	_____	_____	_____	_____
_____	_____	_____	_____	_____

I promise to pray for these 10 unsaved people for two months and invite each of them to our next evangelistic campaign.

_____   _____
Date   Signed

BIG BROTHERS AND BIG SISTERS
"TOP 10" CHECKLIST

Name	Pray for my Top 10 for 60 days	Invite my Top 10 to evangelistic campaign	Did they attend the campaign?	Did they accept Christ?	Have they been invited to local church?	Are they being discipled?	Been invited to membership class?	Been invited to baptism class?	Have they been baptized?	Have they joined the local church?	Are they now a Big Brother/Big Sister?							
Date																		
1.																		
2.																		
3.																		
4.																		
5.																		
6.																		
7.																		
8.																		
9.																		
10.																		

MY COMMITMENT

_____   _____   _____

_____   _____   _____

_____   _____   _____

_____   _____   _____

_____   _____   _____

_____   _____   _____

_____   _____   _____

_____   _____   _____

_____   _____   _____

MY COMMITMENT

_____ _____ _____

_____ _____ _____

_____ _____ _____

_____ _____ _____

_____ _____ _____

_____ _____ _____

_____ _____ _____

_____ _____ _____

_____ _____ _____

_____ _____ _____

_____ _____ _____

Lake View Park
Church of the Nazarene

does hereby recognize

_____

for faithfully developing a relationship with and for winning

to the Lord this year.

Date: _____

Signed: _____

James N. Williams, Senior Pastor

Each One Win One!

Lake View Park
Church of the Nazarene

With God's help and the encouragement and support

of my local congregation, I, _____ ,

commit to winning at least one person to Jesus in 2006.

Signed: _____

(layperson's name)

_____
date

Each One Win One!

Northwest Oklahoma District
Church of the Nazarene

acknowledges that, by faith,

Lake View Park Church of the Nazarene

with the help of the Lord,
will establish a New Church Plant in 2006.

Tharon Daniels, District Superintendent   date

James N. Williams, Senior Pastor   date

Each Church Plant One!

APPENDIX P

"HARVEST NOW"
by Stan Toler

Mark 16:14-20

Question: What is 750,000 miles long, reaches around the earth 30 times, and grows 20 miles longer each day?

The Answer: The line of people who do not know Jesus as Savior!

In India alone, there are half a billion people who have never heard the gospel. I've been to Calcutta. Every day, over 1,000 corpses are taken off its streets, victims of starvation, and almost all of them die without hope. I've watched boatloads of people make their pitiful way to the shore of Hong Kong, seeking freedom and relief from their awful existence. I have traveled up the mighty Amazon River to the edge of the jungles of Bolivia, where people who are one generation out of those jungles desperately need God. I have observed the plight of the Masai warriors in Kenya. I've seen the faraway look in their eyes, as they agonized about meeting the very basic needs of life. I have walked the blighted inner-city streets of Chicago and Los Angeles where little children are more familiar with guns than a living God.

The church of Jesus Christ has an immediate decision to make: It must choose between hiding behind a spiritual fortress or launching out in faith to reach the billions of people in the world who do not have a saving hope in Jesus of Nazareth.

G. B. Williamson described the fortress mentality when he wrote of Christians who "Make the walls higher, lock the doors and focus inward. Become a *sit and look* society of believers, little isles of holiness in the great sea of forgetfulness."

The Challenge of the Harvest (vv. 14-15)

Later Jesus appeared to the Eleven as they were eating; he rebuked them for their lack of faith and their stubborn refusal to believe those who had seen him after he had risen. He said to them, "Go into all the world and preach the good news to all creation."

As Jesus walked the dusty roads of Galilee at harvesttime He passed vast fields of sun-ripened grain. Sent from the Father to be the Savior of the world, His heart must have broken as He compared the grain of those fields to the people He came to redeem. He thought of the throngs (fields) of people into whose hearts the enemy had sown the weeds of selfish rebellion. As Jesus looked over the fields, each kernel of grain must have symbolized their living soul, a soul destined for an eternity apart from God unless the seed of righteousness was planted in their hearts.

1. He taught spiritual truths in parables (Mark 4:26-29).

He also said, "This is what the kingdom of God is like. A man scatters seed on the ground. Night and day, whether he sleeps or gets up, the seed sprouts and grows, though he does not know how. All by itself the soil produces grain—first the stalk, then the head, then the full kernel in the head. As soon as the grain is ripe, he puts the sickle to it, because the harvest has come."

He taught that truth in a parable as the crowds pushed in around Him. Soon they mobbed Jesus until He had to get into a boat and push from the shore.

The harvest had come.

The weeds or wheat would have to be gathered, bundled, and placed where they belonged by virtue of what they were.

Against that awesome inevitability, the Son of God pled with His followers to think of living souls, "The harvest is plentiful, but the workers are few. Ask the Lord of the harvest, therefore, to send out workers into his harvest field" (Luke 10:2).

The harvest had been on His heart from Bethlehem to Calvary.

Following His victorious death and glorious resurrection, Jesus once again reminded His followers about the harvest. Mark wrote that He rebuked His disciples for not launching their faith—for hiding behind their hard-nosed facts instead of trusting in His creative, resurrection power. "He rebuked them for their lack of faith and their stubborn refusal to believe those who had seen him after he had risen" (Mark 16:14).

2. He gave a harvest challenge that has never been withdrawn (v. 15).

He said to them, "Go into all the world and preach the good news to all creation."

It was a challenge that crossed generations. It wasn't just for the disciples, it was for every servant of the Savior—not just for them but for all of us as well.

And it was a worldwide assignment—not a regional one. Anything less than a vision for global evangelism is less than Christ intended.

"All the world."

"To all creation."

Every field.

Every "kernel of grain."

The harvest is now.

No one must be left out. Every single effort that can be made *must* be made to tell every man, woman, boy, or girl about the love of God before it is eternally too late! They must know of that love so vividly expressed in the giving of God's only Son, the Lord Jesus Christ, to save them from the horrors of a death without the hope of heaven.

He told them, "The harvest is plentiful, but the workers are few. Ask the Lord of the harvest, therefore, to send out workers into his harvest field" (Luke 10:2).

The Message of the Harvest (Mark 16:16)

Whoever believes and is baptized will be saved, but whoever does not believe will be condemned.

1. Every person in the world must know the good news of the gospel (John 3:17).

For God did not send his Son into the world to condemn the world, but to save the world through him.

It is a gospel so easily understood that it can be summed up even in just one verse of scripture: John 3:16, "For God so loved the world that he gave his one and only Son, that whoever believes in him shall not perish but have eternal life."

Jesus talked about the importance of knowing this message: "Whoever believes and is baptized will be saved, but whoever does not believe will be condemned" (Mark 16:16).

The harvest is now.

Based on the irrefutable fact of the Word of God, people without Christ are *already* condemned. Already they have a reservation in the place of eternal torment, where the Bible says there is weeping and gnashing of teeth. I believe in a hell because I believe the Bible to be the Word of God. And what He mentions, I must never omit!

Conversely, people who know Christ as their personal Savior are saved already. They *already* have a reserved place in the eternal city of God—a place without sickness, sin, sorrow, strife, or suffering. They have a present-day hope, even though they may be surrounded by the very worst of the world.

The harvest is now.

2. The challenge of the harvest is to share the message of God's love.

Before Jesus ascended into heaven, He gave a commission to His disciples. Matthew wrote it down for us:

All authority in heaven and on earth has been given to me. Therefore go and make disciples of all nations, baptizing them in the name of the Father and of the Son and of the Holy Spirit, and teaching them to obey everything I have commanded you. And surely I am with you always, to the very end of the age (Matt. 28:18-20).

The Promise of the Harvest (Mark 16:17-20)

"And these signs will accompany those who believe: In my name they will drive out demons; they will speak in new tongues; they will pick up snakes with their hands; and when they drink deadly poison, it will not hurt them at all; they will place their hands on sick people, and they will get well."

After the Lord Jesus had spoken to them, he was taken up into heaven and he sat at the right hand of God. Then the disciples went out and preached everywhere, and the Lord worked with them and confirmed his word by the signs that accompanied it.

Granted, the message of the harvest offers a rather narrow view of life, but it has unlimited potential for those who hold it and to those who share it. Fulfilling God's great purpose in the Great Commission has some accompanying and exciting promises.

1. The devices of Satan will be thwarted (v. 17).

In my name they will drive out demons.

ILL. The work of world evangelism is an antidote for evil. As the gospel is preached, the influence of Satan's forces is diminished. Jesus told of the effects of the gospel when He told the story of the demon-possessed man who, after hearing and believing the gospel, was "dressed and in his right mind" (5:15).

2. The preaching of the gospel message will be accompanied by spiritual boldness (16:17).

They will speak in new tongues.

God will open miraculous lines of communication. Barriers of language and culture will be torn down. The message of hope and deliverance will flow like a mighty river—even from the lips of those who are unfamiliar with the language of their hearers. This was exemplified on the Day of Pentecost as people from a myriad of cultures heard the disciples' message in their own language.

The arrival of new technologies to share the old, old story are not coincidental! God will make a way for the people on His planet to hear and see how much He loves them. He will use people like you and me to make a way for guilty, sin-burdened hearts to be set free. He'll break down the walls of language with a Spirit-inspired talent implanted in the mind of a translator.

He'll make a way.

The songwriter said it, "O the love that drew salvation's plan, / O the grace that brought it down to man; / O the mighty gulf that God did span at Calvary."

3. The gospel message will have a healing effect (v. 18).

They will place their hands on sick people and they will get well.

The cause of Christ is wholeness:

The Spirit of the Lord is on me, because he has anointed me to preach good news to the poor. He has sent me to proclaim freedom for the prisoners and recovery of sight for the blind, to release the oppressed (Luke 4:18).

As the apostle Paul wrote, "May God himself, the God of peace, sanctify you through and through. May your whole spirit, soul and body be kept blameless at the coming of our Lord Jesus Christ" (1 Thess. 5:23).

The gospel not only has power to transform the soul but transforms the mind and the body as well. That's a message for this day! AIDS is crippling our society and leaving orphans abandoned on city streets. Addiction to drugs has almost wiped out an entire generation. Demon powers are wrestling sanity away from the minds of anxious millions. Selfish authorities have stockpiled foods in the world's warehouses while tiny bodies bloat from malnutrition and disease.

The harvest is now.

The gospel must be preached in order for its positive effect to impact our world.

Whatever it takes, we must take the gospel to the people!

The Lord of the Harvest (Mark 16:19)

After the Lord Jesus had spoken to them, he was taken up into heaven and he sat at the right hand of God.

1. Every ministry comes under His loving care.

It is a word portrait that sets our soul on fire! The same Jesus who was reviled *on earth* now rules *over the earth!*

The harvest is now.

But evangelistic organizations are not in charge of this harvest. Christ is. From His throne in heaven He appoints, equips, and inspects the ministry of His people.

2. Earthly organizations are merely service agencies that fulfill His great cause in the world.

And people who administer those organizations answer directly to their Head, the Lord Jesus Christ himself.

The Example of the Harvest (v. 20)

Then the disciples went out and preached everywhere, and the Lord worked with them and confirmed his word by the signs that accompanied it.

1. There is always room for one more in the Kingdom.

The Acts of the Apostles were acts of evangelism and discipleship. And their numbers grew daily. What began with 120 is now over 2 billion and still growing! But the followers of Christ were never content with their numbers. That's because the army of Christ has always been on a soul-saving mission. "Then the disciples went out and preached everywhere, and the Lord worked with them and confirmed his word by the signs that accompanied it" (v. 20). They went everywhere with the belief that there is always room for one more in the Kingdom. That philosophy of ministry comes from the very heart of a Savior who talked of the search for one lost sheep, one lost coin, or one lost son.

Jesus said this good news of hope must be preached to every soul. It must not be catalogued and stored in some climate-controlled vault. It must be tossed about like seed to the land.

- It must be preached from pulpits.
- It must be transcribed to audio.
- It must be produced on film and DVD.
- It must be broadcast on the Internet.
- It must be shared in small groups.
- It must be translated and printed for people of every language to understand.
- It must be told one-to-one.

2. The seed must be sown in the hearts of the weary and the waiting.

The Urgency of the Harvest (John 4:35)

Do you not say, "Four months more and then the harvest"? I tell you, open your eyes and look at the fields! They are ripe for harvest.

The harvest is now.

ILL. The unsaved must be saved now.

Believers must be Spirit-filled now.

New converts must be discipled and equipped for service now.

Churches must be planted now.

But that will not happen without the mass mobilization of Christians. And that can happen in several ways. For example, there are at least three things that Christians must do *now* to reach the world's billions.

1. Impacting the world begins with intercession (Matt. 9:38).

Ask the Lord of the harvest, therefore, to send out workers into his harvest field.

If people are going to be saved over there, then someone over here must be serious about his or her prayer life. Someone will put a world map before himself or herself and cry out to God on behalf of people in each of the countries on the map who don't know Jesus.

Someone will forego a meal and pray that someone else will discover the Bread of Life. Someone will get on his or her knees so that someone else will be able to get on his or her feet. Someone will pause for a moment during a workday to think about a Christian worker halfway around the world who needs a touch from God.

The harvest is now. Someone must pray.

2. Investing in souls reaps eternal benefits (Luke 12:33).

Sell your possessions and give to the poor. Provide purses for yourselves that will not wear out, a treasure in heaven that will not be exhausted, where no thief comes near and no moth destroys.

Jesus said, "Sell your possessions and give to the poor. Provide purses for yourselves that will not wear out, a treasure in heaven that will not be exhausted, where no thief comes near and no moth destroys." Jesus taught His disciples that following Him meant sacrificing the immediate for the cause of the eternal. What they gave was actually an investment.

God has asked us to give out of the abundance that He has given to us. The more He gives, the more we can give. It's a very familiar promise. Jesus said, "Give, and it will be given to you. A good measure, pressed down, shaken together and running over, will be poured into your lap. For with the measure you use, it will be measured to you" (6:38).

The harvest is now. Someone needs to give.

3. Reaching our world involves a willingness to *go*.

Jesus said, "You did not choose me, but I chose you and appointed you to *go* and bear fruit—fruit that will last. Then the Father will give you whatever you ask in my name" (John 15:16, emphasis mine). Citizens of the Kingdom aren't appointed to sit, they're appointed to serve. Jesus rebuked the Eleven for their closed-door and shuttered-windows approach to ministry. There was no time for them to sit in their coffee klatches and discuss the "whethers" or "nots" of His triumph over the grave. The message of the Resurrection needed an immediate audience!

It's the same today. Ripened fields need on-site harvesters not workers who lounge around the dining table. There's a *g-o* in *go*spel and Jesus put it there!

Global evangelism is a wonderful opportunity for anyone—in any stage of a career or in retirement. The wisdom and skills that brought you to this point are those that the Lord of the harvest can use to bring the lost to His kingdom.

The harvest is now. Someone needs to apply for a passport.

It may be that the only voyage you've ever taken has been on a guilt trip. But this isn't about guilt trips. It's about the gospel. It's about laying everything dear to you, including your very life, on an altar of sacrifice. It's about praying that the Lord of the harvest would include you in the harvest.

Written on the hard hat of a rescue worker who fought valiantly to rescue people from the bombed Murrah government building in Oklahoma City on that April day in 1995 are these words: "I only wish we could have done more."

The harvest is now.

Across the street or across the seas, people need the message that so many of us have taken for granted. Our hearts have been callused by too much truth. We've sung too many tunes while most of the world doesn't have a melody.

—Stan Toler

APPENDIX Q

MEMBERSHIP CLASS OUTLINE

Belonging
to the
Lake View Park Family Tree

Membership Class

"I am the vine, you are the branches.
If a man remains in me and I in him,
he will bear much fruit;
apart from me you can do nothing."
John 15:5 (NIV)

"I am the Vine, you are the branches.
When you're joined with me and I with you,
the relation intimate and organic,
the harvest is sure to be abundant.
Separated, you can't produce a thing."
John 15:5 (TM)

Lake View Park Church of the Nazarene

OUR MISSION

We are a Christ-centered Body of Believers established on the Word of God, focused on the needs of our community and the world. We have no greater call than to know Him, to be known by Him, and to lead others to Him.

OUR VISION

To be a New Testament church, fueled by prayer, fed by the Word of God, empowered by the Holy Spirit so that we might fulfill Scripture and see the Lord add to our number daily those who are being saved.

OUR GOALS

Children's Ministry
Financial Peace
Missions Focus
Renewal Focus

We must become a river and not a reservoir!

Lake View Park's "Ships" of Ministry

LEADERSHIP
- ► Vision/Mission
- ► Preaching
- ► Intern Ministry
- ► Mentoring Leaders
- ► Leadership Training
- ► Follow-up Assimilation
- ► Pastor's Welcome Class
- ► Spiritual Gifts Discovery
- ► Discipleship Classes

PARTNERSHIP
- ► Building and Properties

FRIENDSHIP
- ► Prayer Ministry
- ► Encouragement
- ► Evangelism (events and training)
- ► Unchurched Events

FELLOWSHIP
- ► Sunday School Ministry
- ► Children
- ► Youth (Nazarene Youth International)
- ► Adults
- ► Senior Adults
- ► Women's Ministry
- ► Men's Ministry
- ► Athletics
- ► Weddings/Showers
- ► Missions (Nazarene Missions International)

WORSHIP
- ► Worship Services
- ► Music
- ► Special Celebrations
- ► Baptism
- ► Communion
- ► Audiovisual
- ► Decorations
- ► Hospitality and All Church Dinner Events

STEWARDSHIP
- ► Budget Preparation
- ► Regulation and Review
- ► Recording and Reporting
- ► Audits
- ► Stewardship Emphasis
- ► Fund-raising
- ► Business Operations
- ► Counting Teams
- ► Financial Contributions

Lake View Park's Core Values

1. We value the souls of lost people everywhere.

2. We value spending intimate time with a personal God in personal and corporate prayer.

3. We value the Word of God.

4. We value a lifestyle of holiness empowered by the Holy Spirit.

5. We value authentic relationship with God's family.

6. We value the worship of God, both personally and corporately.

7. We value the unique gifts of God's people.

8. We value personal integrity and honesty.

Lake View Park's Statement of Belief

Lake View Park is a member of the Church of the Nazarene. We have 16 Articles of Faith. These statements are given in their completeness in our church *Manual.* It takes many hours of intense study to understand all the theological terms used in the Articles of Faith. Because a statement of doctrine is meant to last for many generations, it is necessary to present it in the precise and technical language of theology. Here is a summary of these 16 statements:

1. We believe in one God, the Creator of all things, who reveals himself as Father, Son, and Spirit. (Triune God)

2. We believe in Jesus Christ, who is fully God and fully human at the same time, who became like us to bring about our salvation. (Jesus Christ)

3. We believe in the Holy Spirit, who is active in the world, bringing man to salvation. (The Holy Spirit)

4. We believe that the Bible is the Word of God, giving us all we need to know about how to be saved. (The Holy Scriptures)

5. We believe that we are all sinners by both nature and act and need God's forgiveness and cleansing. (Sin, Original and Personal)

6. We believe that Jesus Christ died on the Cross and that, trusting in His death, we can be restored to right relationship with God. (Atonement)

7. We believe that God has enabled us to turn to Him from sin, but that He has not forced us to do so. (Prevenient Grace)

8. We believe that individually we must repent, turn away from our sins, and trust Christ to accept us. (Repentance)

9. We believe that when we turn from sin and trust in Christ, the old record of sin is wiped clean, and we are born anew, thus becoming part of the family of God. (Justification, Regeneration, Adoption)

10. We believe that after being born anew, we need the fullness of God's Spirit in our hearts. When we make a complete commitment to Him (consecration), He cleanses our spirit, fills us with His perfect love, and gives us the power to live victoriously. (Sanctification)

11. We believe in the Church, the community that confesses Jesus Christ as Lord. (Church)

12. We believe in baptism and urge people to be baptized as Christians. (Baptism)

13. We believe in the Lord's Supper. (Lord's Supper)

14. We believe God can heal. We pray for healing. We also believe that God can work through medical science. (Divine Healing)

15. We believe that Jesus Christ is coming again. (Second Coming)

16. We believe that everyone shall face the judgment of God with its rewards and punishments. (Resurrection, Judgment and Destiny)

A statement of belief has little value without the action of believing.

To believe is to trust God, to trust Him with complete obedience.

What Does Lake View Park Ask of Me?

To Prepare for Ministry

▷ by discovering my gifts and talents

▷ by being equipped by my pastors and teachers (1 Pet. 4:10)

Each one should use whatever gift he has received to serve others, faithfully administering God's grace in its various forms.

▷ by seeking the mind and heart of Christ (Phil. 2:3-4, 7)

Do nothing out of selfish ambition or vain conceit, but in humility consider others better than yourselves. Each of you should look not only to your own interests, but also to the interests of others . . . but made of himself nothing, taking the very nature of a servant, being made in human likeness.

To Share the Responsibility

▷ by praying for the growth and health of the Church (Eph. 1:16)

I have not stopped giving thanks for you, remembering you in my prayers.

▷ by attending faithfully (Heb. 10:25)

Let us not give up meeting together, as some are in the habit of doing, but let us encourage one another—and all the more as you see the Day approaching.

▷ by inviting my unchurched friends and relatives (Luke 14:23)

Then the master told his servant, "Go out to the roads and country lanes and make them come in, so that my house will be full."

▷ by sharing a powerful example (1 Pet. 2:12)

Live such good lives among the pagans that, though they accuse you of doing wrong, they may see your good deeds and glorify God on the day he visits us.

▷ by giving regularly, generously, and cheerfully (Mal. 3:10)

Bring the whole tithe into the storehouse, that there may be food in my house. "Test me in this," says the LORD Almighty, "and see if I will not throw open the floodgates of heaven and pour out so much blessing that you will not have room enough for it."

To Care for Others

▷ **by loving the family of God (1 Pet. 1:22)**

Now that you have purified yourselves by obeying the truth so that you have sincere love for your brothers, love one another deeply, from the heart.

▷ **by building up, not tearing down (Eph. 4:29)**

Do not let any unwholesome talk come out of your mouths, but only what is helpful for building others up according to their needs, that it may benefit those who listen.

▷ **by using my gifts and talents (1 Pet. 4:10)**

Each one should use whatever gift he has received to serve others, faithfully administering God's grace in its various forms.

Lake View Park's Insights into Spiritual Gifts

To whom and how are spiritual gifts given?

1. Every believer is spiritually gifted (1 Pet. 4:10; 1 Cor. 12:7; Eph. 4:7-8)

2. When he or she becomes a Christian (1 Cor. 12:13)

3. With the gift(s) that God chooses for him or her (1 Cor. 12:11, 18)

> *Note:* No one Christian has all the gifts nor is any one gift common to all Christians. (1 Cor. 12:12-18)

What is the purpose of spiritual gifts?

1. The glory of God and His Church (1 Pet. 4:10-11)

2. The building up of the Body of Christ (Eph. 4:12)

3. The unity of the Body (Eph. 4:13)

4. The maturity of the Body (Eph. 4:14-15)

5. The growth of the Body (Eph. 4:16)

6. The common good of the Body (Eph. 4:16)

LAKE VIEW PARK

What are the differences between *human talents* and *spiritual gifts*?

Talents	Gifts
1. Inherited from forefathers	1. Given by the Holy Spirit
2. Present from natural birth	2. Present from new birth
3. God-given to all members of the human race	3. God-given to members of Christ's Body
4. For human activities	4. For ministry of the Body
5. Can be operated independent of the Holy Spirit	5. Dependent on the Holy Spirit
6. Ministers primarily on a natural level	6. Ministers on a spiritual level
7. Effects are usually temporal/finite	7. Effects are eternal/infinite
8. Glorifies self	8. Glorifies God

What are the differences between the fruit of the Spirit and the gifts of the Spirit?

Fruit	Gifts
1. Defines what a Christian is	1. Determines what a Christian does
2. Same in every Christian	2. Different in each Christian
3. Singular	3. Plural
4. Satan cannot imitate	4. Satan can imitate
5. Deals with character	5. Deals with service ministry
6. End in itself	6. Means to an end
7. Permanent/Eternal	7. Will cease
8. According to spirituality and maturity	8. Not according to spirituality

Lake View Park "Footprints"

Lake View Park Church of the Nazarene was organized on August 7, 1955, with the Rev. J. T. Gassett officiating, beginning with 75 charter members. Dr. R. T. Williams and his staff from Oklahoma City First Church of the Nazarene held services at the chapel for the first three months.

Rev. Frank J. Kemendo, the first regular pastor, begin his work at Lake View Park on June 19, 1955. During his pastorate, an addition on the north side of the chapel provided some classrooms. In the spring of 1958, Rev. Kemendo accepted a call to pastor in Port Arthur, Texas.

In August 1958, Rev. Bill Draper, a staff member of Oklahoma City First Church, accepted the pastoral call to Lake View Park. Under his leadership the young church grew and annexes were added for Sunday School and office space and a new sanctuary was dedicated. Pastor Draper left Lake View to become assistant to the president of Mid-America Nazarene College in January 1967.

Rev. J. V. Morsch became the new pastor of Lake View in January 1967. Growth continued until it was necessary to have simultaneous double worship and Sunday School services. Two adjacent homes were purchased and two sanctuary entrances were added for more seating capacity, in place of the original north entrance. In 1970, Pastor Morsch became pastor of Nashville First Church.

Rev. Ed Murphey became our new pastor in 1970. During his pastorate, a new four-bedroom parsonage was purchased as well as two more houses for expansion of the church property. The house at the corner of 50th and Cromwell was remodeled for church office space. In April 1972, Rev. Murphey and several Lake View members organized Community Church of the Nazarene, which is now Metroplex Fellowship Church of the Nazarene.

Rev. Jim Bond began his pastorate at Lake View in July 1972. Under his leadership the church bought more houses on north Cromwell and a new addition to the church was built, including a nursery, Sunday School rooms, a fellowship hall, kitchen, and gymnasium. Rev. Bond left Lake View to assume responsibilities as pastor of Colorado Springs First Church in 1975.

At the 20th anniversary banquet and new building dedication, Rev. Wallace Renegar was welcomed as our new pastor. The year was 1975. And during his service among us the sanctuary platform and the barracks were remodeled. A new sanctuary sound system was installed; an annual Thanksgiving dinner for the poor was held; we began Wednesday night family dinners; and an adult retreat was begun. Pastor Renegar moved to First Church of the Nazarene in Santa Cruz, California, in 1978.

Rev. Howard Rickey became Lake View's pastor in 1978. During his pastorship, CLIP (Christian Laymen in Partnership) was begun. Land was purchased at Northwest 164th and MacArthur through the selling of shares, with plans to deed 30 acres to the church and eventually build a debt-free church on the site. Rev. Rickey resigned as pastor in April of 1981.

In September 1981, Rev. Jerry Baker came to Lake View from Charlotte, North Carolina. The church office was moved to 3500 Northwest 50 to make way for the expansion of what is now Lake Hefner Parkway. Lake View Academy moved into our facilities in time to start classes in the fall of 1982. In 1985 CLIP officially deeded 30 acres of debt-free land to the church. Dedication services were held on the site underneath a large tent on Sunday, June 2, 1985. An architectural rendering of the site plan and church facilities were drawn. Shortly after this time, Oklahoma City was hit hard by the oil "bust," and Lake View Park had many families move out of state to find new jobs. The decision was made to remain at this location, retaining the northwest property for future consideration. In the fall of 1988 Rev. Baker became the pastor of University Boulevard Church of the Nazarene in Jacksonville, Florida.

Rev. Harold (Hal) Perkins arrived as Lake View's new pastor in April 1989. During his tenure, enrollment at Lake View Academy increased and classes were expanded. Updates and remodeling of the facility were done: new floor in the fellowship hall; new carpet in the sanctuary and foyers. In the late 1980s, the academy board began to look at other facilities so they could continue their growth and ministry to students. One of the most significant events in the life of Lake View Park started out like any other summer youth outreach program. In the summer of 1991, our youth went into a blighted area just south of downtown Oklahoma City, where they cleaned yards, painted houses, cut down underbrush, and worked on the property of Central Church of the Nazarene. A daytime Bible school was held for area children and evening evangelistic services were held. Their enthusiasm drew many adults into the week-long project. Out of this summer ministry, Love Link Ministries was born and is now an established ministry of the Church of the Nazarene. Rev. Perkins resigned in September 1998 to become senior pastor of Seattle North Church of the Nazarene.

After a full year without a pastor, Lake View welcomed Rev. James (Jim) Williams in August 1999. In April 2000 we formally adopted the Mixtecos of Huitepec, an unreached people group in the state of Oaxaca, Mexico. We have joined in a covenant with two other Nazarene churches to pray, give, and go so that a Christ-centered church can be established in their village. It was a wonderful day of commitment and celebration, uniting Oklahoma City Segunda Iglesia and Oaxaca City Segunda Iglesia with Lake View Park. Shortly thereafter, in May 2000, Lake View Park celebrated its 45th anniversary with a weekend of reunion activities to celebrate God's faithfulness to this local church.

The two main foyers of the sanctuary were completely remodeled and refurnished just in time for the 45th anniversary. Lake View Academy relocated in the summer of 2000. Sadly, the school has since closed its doors. The original chapel building has been refreshed for use as Sunday School rooms. The nursery area was completely remodeled; Promise Land now welcomes young children to a bright, clean, and safe environment. The fellowship hall and kitchen have been completely updated and serve as a wonderful center for Christian community. Plans are being set forth to remodel the children's ministry area, complete with new furniture and state-of-the-art technology.

God has been bringing in new people almost every week. We are committed, as a congregation, to living out our mission and vision statements as we pledge ourselves to follow God's leading.

Getting to Know Us at Lake View Park
The Church of the Nazarene . . . a Brief History

Following is a summary of the history of the Church of the Nazarene. A more detailed version is available online at http://www.nazarene.org/archives/history/index.html.

The Holiness Movement of the 19th Century. In the 19th century a renewed emphasis on Christian Holiness began in the Eastern United States and spread throughout the nation. Timothy Merritt, Methodist clergyman and founding editor of the *Guide to Christian Perfection,* was among the leaders of the Holiness revival. The central figure of the movement was Phoebe Palmer of New York City, leader of the Tuesday Meeting for the Promotion of Holiness, at which Methodist bishops, educators, and other clergy joined the original group of women in seeking holiness. During four decades Mrs. Palmer promoted the Methodist phase of the Holiness Movement through public speaking, writing, and as editor of the influential *Guide to Holiness.*

The Holiness revival spilled outside the bounds of Methodism. Charles G. Finney and Asa Mahan, both of Oberlin College, led the renewed emphasis on holiness in Presbyterian and Congregationalist circles, as did revivalist William Boardman. Baptist evangelist A. B. Earle was among the leaders of the Holiness Movement within his denomination. Hannah Whitall Smith, a Quaker and popular holiness revivalist, published *The Christian's Secret of a Happy Life* (1875), a classic text in Christian spirituality.

In 1867 Methodist ministers John A. Wood, John Inskip, and others began at Vineland, New Jersey, the first of a long series of national camp meetings. They also organized at that time the National Camp Meeting Association for the Promotion of Holiness, commonly known as the National Holiness Association (now the Christian Holiness Partnership). Until the early years of the 20th century, this organization sponsored Holiness camp meetings throughout the United States. Local and regional Holiness associations also appeared, and a vital Holiness press published many periodicals and books.

Q14

The witness to Christian Holiness played roles of varying significance in the founding of the Wesleyan Methodist Church (1843), the Free Methodist Church (1860), and, in England, the Salvation Army (1865). In the 1880s new distinctively Holiness churches sprang into existence, including the Church of God (Anderson, Indiana) and the Church of God (Holiness). Several older religious traditions were also influenced by the Holiness Movement, including certain groups of Mennonites, Brethren, and Friends that adopted the Wesleyan-Holiness view of entire sanctification. The Brethren in Christ Church and the Evangelical Friends Alliance are examples of this blending of spiritual traditions.

Uniting of Holiness Groups

In the 1890s a new wave of independent Holiness entities came into being. These included independent churches, urban missions, rescue homes, and missionary and evangelistic associations. Some of the people involved in these organizations yearned for union into a national Holiness church. Out of that impulse the present-day Church of the Nazarene was born.

The Association of Pentecostal Churches of America. On July 21, 1887, the People's Evangelical Church was organized with 51 members at Providence, Rhode Island, with Fred A. Hillery as pastor. The following year the Mission Church at Lynn, Massachusetts, was organized with C. Howard Davis as pastor. On March 13 and 14, 1890, representatives from these and other independent Holiness congregations met at Rock, Massachusetts, and organized the Central Evangelical Holiness Association with churches in Rhode Island, New Hampshire, and Massachusetts. In 1892, the Central Evangelical Holiness Association ordained Anna S. Hanscombe, believed to be the first of many women ordained to the Christian ministry in the parent bodies of the Church of the Nazarene.

In January 1894 businessman William Howard Hoople founded a Brooklyn mission, reorganized the following May as Utica Avenue Pentecostal Tabernacle. By the end of the following year, Bedford Avenue Pentecostal Church and Emmanuel Pentecostal Tabernacle were also organized. In December 1895, delegates from these three congregations adopted a constitution, a summary of doctrines, and bylaws, forming the Association of Pentecostal Churches of America.

On November 12, 1896, a joint committee of the Central Evangelical Holiness Association and the Association of Pentecostal Churches of America met in Brooklyn and framed a plan of union, retaining the name of the latter for the united body. Prominent workers in this denomination were Hiram F. Reynolds, H. B. Hosley, C. Howard Davis, William Howard Hoople, and, later, E. E. Angell. Some of these were originally lay preachers who were later ordained as ministers by their congregations. This church was decidedly missionary, and under the leadership of Hiram F. Reynolds, missionary secretary, embarked upon an ambitious program of Christian witness to the Cape Verde Islands, India, and other places. *The Beulah Christian* was published as its official paper.

The Holiness Church of Christ. In July 1894 R. L. Harris organized the New Testament Church of Christ at Milan, Tennessee, shortly before his death. Mary Lee Cagle, widow of R. L. Harris, continued the work and became its most prominent early leader. This church, strictly congregational in polity, spread throughout Arkansas and western Texas, with scattered congregations in Alabama and Missouri. Mary Cagle and a coworker, Mrs. E. J. Sheeks, were ordained in 1899 in the first class of ordinands.

Beginning in 1888 a handful of congregations bearing the name the Holiness Church were organized in Texas by ministers Thomas and Dennis Rogers, who came from California.

In 1901 the first congregation of the Independent Holiness Church was formed at Van Alstyne, Texas, by Charles B. Jernigan. At an early date, James B. Chapman affiliated with this denomination, which prospered and grew rapidly. In time, the congregations led by Dennis Rogers affiliated with the Independent Holiness Church.

In November 1904 representatives of the New Testament Church of Christ and the Independent Holiness Church met at Rising Star, Texas, where they agreed upon principles of union, adopted a *Manual,* and chose the name Holiness Church of Christ. This union was finalized the following year at a delegated general council held at Pilot Point, Texas. The *Holiness Evangel* was the church's official paper. Its other leading ministers included William E. Fisher, J. D. Scott, and J. T. Upchurch. Among its key lay leaders were Edwin H. Sheeks, R. B. Mitchum, and Mrs. Donie Mitchum.

Several leaders of this church were active in the Holiness Association of Texas, a vital interdenominational body that sponsored a college at Peniel, near Greenville, Texas. The association also sponsored the *Pentecostal Advocate,* the Southwest's leading Holiness paper, which became a Nazarene organ in 1910. E. C. DeJernett, a minister, and C. A. McConnell, a layman, were prominent workers in this organization.

The Church of the Nazarene. In October 1895 Phineas F. Bresee, D.D., and Joseph P. Widney, M.D., with about 100 others, including Alice P. Baldwin, Leslie F. Gay, W. S. and Lucy P. Knott, C. E. McKee, and members of the Bresee and Widney families, organized the Church of the Nazarene at Los Angeles. At the outset they saw this church as the first of a denomination that preached the reality of entire sanctification received through faith in Christ. They held that Christians sanctified by faith should follow Christ's example and preach the gospel to the poor. They felt called especially to this work. They believed that unnecessary elegance and adornment of houses of worship did not represent the spirit of Christ but the spirit of the world and that their expenditures of time and money should be given to Christlike ministries for the salvation of souls and the relief of the needy. They organized the church accordingly. They adopted general rules, a statement of belief, a polity based on a limited superintendency, procedures for the consecration of deaconesses and the ordination of elders, and a ritual. These were published as a *Manual* beginning in 1898. They published a paper known as *The Nazarene* and then *The Nazarene Messenger.* The Church of the Nazarene spread chiefly along the West Coast, with scattered congregations east of the Rocky Mountains as far as Illinois.

Among the ministers who cast their lot with the new church were H. D. Brown, W. E. Shepard, C. W. Ruth, L. B. Kent, Isaiah Reid, J. B. Creighton, C. E. Cornell, Robert Pierce, and W. C. Wilson. Among the first to be ordained by the new church were Joseph P. Widney himself, Elsie and DeLance Wallace, Lucy P. Knott, and E. A. Girvin.

Phineas F. Bresee's 38 years' experience as a pastor, superintendent, editor, college board member, and camp meeting preacher in Methodism, and his unique personal magnetism, entered into the ecclesiastical statesmanship that he brought to the merging of the several Holiness churches into a national body.

The Year of Uniting: 1907-8. The Association of Pentecostal Churches of America, the Church of the Nazarene, and the Holiness Church of Christ were brought into association with one another by C. W. Ruth, assistant general superintendent of the Church of the Nazarene, who had extensive friendships throughout the Wesleyan-Holiness Movement. Delegates of the Association of Pentecostal Churches of America and the Church of the Nazarene convened in general assembly at Chicago, from October 10 to 17, 1907. The merging groups agreed upon a church government that balanced the need for a superintendency with the independence of local congregations. Superintendents were to foster and care for churches already established and were to organize and encourage the organizing of churches everywhere, but their authority was not to interfere with the independent actions of a fully organized church. Further, the General Assembly adopted a name for the united body drawn from both organizations: The Pentecostal Church of the Nazarene. Phineas F. Bresee and Hiram F. Reynolds were elected general superintendents. A delegation of observers from the Holiness Church of Christ was present and participated in the assembly work.

During the following year, two other accessions occurred. In April 1908 P. F. Bresee organized a congregation of the Pentecostal Church of the Nazarene at Peniel, Texas, which brought into the church leading figures in the Holiness Association of Texas and paved the way for other members to join. In September, the Pennsylvania Conference of the Holiness Christian Church, after receiving a release from its General Conference, dissolved itself and under the leadership of H. G. Trumbaur united with the Pentecostal Church of the Nazarene.

The second General Assembly of the Pentecostal Church of the Nazarene met in a joint session with the General Council of the Holiness Church of Christ from October 8 to 14, 1908, at Pilot Point, Texas. The year of uniting ended on Tuesday morning, October 13, when R. B. Mitchum moved and C. W. Ruth seconded the proposition: "That the union of the two churches be now consummated." Several spoke favorably on the motion. Phineas Bresee had exerted continual effort toward this proposed outcome. At 10:40 A.M., amid great enthusiasm, the motion to unite was adopted by a unanimous rising vote.

Denominational Change of Name. The General Assembly of 1919, in response to memorials from 35 district assemblies, officially changed the name of the organization to Church of the Nazarene because of new meanings that had become associated with the term *Pentecostal.*

Toward a Global Church

The world areas where the church has entered reached a total of 138 by 2001. Thousands of ministers and lay workers have indigenized the Church of the Nazarene in their respective cultures, thereby contributing to the mosaic of national identities that form our international communion.

Distinctives of International Ministry. Historically, Nazarene global ministry has centered around evangelism, compassionate ministry, and education. The evangelistic impulse was exemplified in the lives of H. F. Schmelzenbach, L. S. Tracy, Esther Carson Winans, Samuel Krikorian, and others whose names symbolize this dimension of ministry. Around the world, Nazarene churches and districts continue to reflect a revivalistic and evangelistic character.

The international roots of Nazarene compassionate ministry lie in early support for famine relief and orphanage work in India. This impulse was strengthened by the Nazarene Medical Missionary Union, organized in the early 1920s to build Bresee Memorial Hospital in Tamingfu, China. An extensive medical work has developed in Swaziland, and other compassionate ministries have developed around the world.

Education is an aspect of world ministry exemplified early by Hope School for Girls, founded in Calcutta by Mrs. Sukhoda Banarji in 1905 and adopted the following year by the Church of the Nazarene. Outside North America, Nazarenes have established schools for primary education and for specialized ministerial training. There are graduate seminaries in the Philippines and the United States; liberal arts institutions in Africa, Korea, and the United States; one junior college in Japan; two nursing schools in India and Papua New Guinea; and over 40 Bible/theological institutions around the world.

The church has prospered as these components of its mission have developed. In 2001 the Church of the Nazarene had an international membership of 1,390,306, distributed in over 12,600 congregations.

As a result of this historical development, the denomination is poised today with an unfinished agenda of moving from international presence to an international community of faith. Recognition of this fact led the 1976 General Assembly to authorize a Commission on Internationalization, whose report to the 1980 General Assembly led to the creation of a system of world region areas. The number and boundaries of the original world regions have since changed. The current ones are: the Africa Region, the Asia-Pacific Region, the Canada Region, the Caribbean Region, the Eurasia Region, the Mexico-Central America Region, the South America Region, and eight regions in the United States.

—Nazarene *Manual* 2001-5

NOTES

Chapter 1

1. Barna Research Group, *Never on a Sunday: The Challenge of the Unchurched* (Glendale, Calif.: Barna Research Group, 1990), 12.
2. George O. Hunter III, *To Spread the Power* (Nashville: Abingdon Press, 1987), 102.
3. Ibid., 103.

Chapter 2

1. Kenneth Scott Latourette, *A History of Christianity* (New York: Harper and Row, 1975), 204.

Chapter 4

1. Barna Research Group, *Never on a Sunday,* 24.

Chapter 5

1. This plan was used by Dr. Luis Palau's crusade team. It was created by Rev. John McWilliams and implemented by Rev. Vidal Valencia. We thank them for this important contribution to the Kingdom.

Chapter 6

1. Kenneth Crow and Dale Jones, Research Division, Church of the Nazarene, 1997.

Chapter 7

1. In 1991 in Quito, Ecuador, there were 267 unchurched people who accepted Christ in a three-day campaign; in Rosario, Argentina, there were 162 in two days; and in Cali, Colombia, there were 195.
2. Barna Research Group, *Never on a Sunday,* 28.